D1377626

GIANTS
OF THE SEA

WHALES, DOLPHINS, AND THEIR HABITS

THOMASSON-GRANT
CHARLOTTESVILLE, VIRGINIA

CONTENTS

Text by
Gaetano Cafiero
Maddalena Jahoda

Edited by
Valeria Manferto

Designed by
Patrizia Balocco

Illustrations by
Monica Falcone

Translated by
Anthony Shuggar

RIGHT
Pilot whales, also known as blackfish, are easily recognizable by the blunt shape of their heads.

FACING PAGE
Their knobby snouts and long flippers make these humpback whales easy to identify.

*Published 1993 by Thomasson-Grant, One Morton Drive, Charlottesville, Virginia, 22903-6806.
World copyright © 1993 Edizioni White Star, Via Candido Sassone 22/24, Vercelli, Italy.*

Photography copyright as credited on page 144.

*Color separations by Magenta Lithographic Co., Singapore
Printed and bound by Legatoria Lego SpA, Vicenza, Italy*

00 99 98 97 96 95 94 93 5 4 3 2 1

Library of Congress Cataloging-in-Publication Data

*Cafiero, Gaetano, 1937-
  [Balene. English]
  Giants of the sea : whales, dolphins, and their habits / [text by Gaetano Cafiero, Maddalena Jahoda ; edited by Valeria Manferto ; translated by Anthony Shuggar].
    p. cm.
   ISBN 1-56566-046-3
   1. Cetacea. 2. Killer whale.
3. Dolphins. I. Jahoda, Maddalena. II. Manferto, Valeria. III. Title.
QL737.C4C2413 1993
599.5--dc20   93-28091
                CIP*

PAGES 2-3
Humpback whales leaping out of the water always provide a spectacular show.

PAGES 4-5
Fin whales can swallow as much as a ton of herring each day.

PAGES 6-7
Sperm whales hold the world mammalian record for staying under water. They can swim as deep as 6,500 feet.

PAGES 10-11
A group of spotted dolphins swim along with customary elegance.

PAGES 12-13
For many years, killer whales were wrongly accused of attacking humans.

PREFACE

FACING, UPPER

The common dolphin is one of the most gregarious of the various cetacean species. A school may be composed of hundreds of individuals.

FACING, LOWER

The dolphins of the family Stenella *are a group of dolphins that include at least five different species; concerning the exact subdivision of these species, however, scientists are not in perfect agreement. At times, the coloring varies greatly from one population to the next. This is the case, for instance, with the striped dolphins, one of the species that is most easily identifiable. In the eastern Pacific (but not elsewhere), the spotted and striped dolphins are among those cetaceans that, for reasons that remain unknown, swim in the company of huge schools of tuna. The fishermen take advantage of this remarkable partnership; they spot dolphins and thus locate the tuna and surround them with their trawling nets; unfortunately, by so doing, they claim a number of victims among the dolphins. In order to discourage this mass slaughter, the United States and a number of other nations boycott the tuna caught in this manner.*

Cetacea is the order into which naturalists have placed mammals that least comfortably fit the characteristics of their class, both in terms of habitat and anatomical structure. Cetacean—first in Latin, and later in English—comes from the Greek *keté*, which is a blanket term for sea monster. Aristotle summarily considered the cetaceans to be *keté*, but the Greek philosopher, the first of the naturalists, was not familiar with the techniques of anatomical dissection, and so it was not until the sixteenth century that the true nature of the order was discovered. Almost two millennia after Aristotle, two illustrious French naturalists—Guillaume Rondelet and Pierre Belon—examined a dolphin "from within." The results of their examination were published in 1551 in the *Histoire Naturelle des Estranges Poissons Marins*; in this book, the two naturalists speak with impatience of "those modern authors who describe the nature of animals and plants with which they are not familiar." Belon emphasized, "I have never written anything that I have not myself seen." At the end of the *Histoire*, however, the dolphin remained a "strange fish." And in the imagination of the masses, whales and their cousins continued to be considered as *keté*, or sea monsters. Imagine the ideas most people had (and in some cases still have today) about the inhabitants of the oceans, and especially those denizens of the deep that suddenly explode upon the surface with their immense bodies, clouding the air with mighty blasts of misty breath, slicing the water with tall, straight, and menacing fins—then disappear into the abyss, down into unimaginable depths.

The shape of cetaceans seems to be the source of their name, at least in English. *Whale* is a generic term covering the two cetacean groups toothed and baleen whales. Herman Melville devotes part of the introduction to his masterpiece, *Moby Dick*, or *The White Whale*, to the matter of the word's etymology. He cites the Greek and Latin words, passing then to the Anglo-Saxon term *whoel*, and onward to the Danish term *hvalt*, the Swedish *hwal*, the Dutch *wal*, the Icelandic *whale*, the Spanish *ballena*, the French *baleine*, and even the Fijian term *peki-nui-nui*. He relied on Webster's dictionary: "This animal is named from roundness or rolling; for in Danish *hvalt* is arched or vaulted."

In the tale of Jonah, the whale could be said to represent an ark: when the prophet is swallowed, he enters the intermediate obscurity between two stages of existence; when the whale spits him out, he is reborn to new life. Similar myths exist in Africa, in Polynesia, and in Lap-

land—in which someone enters the belly of a monster, generally a sea monster, and then emerges from the shadows having undergone a rite of passage or initiation. Here, we can clearly see the evil aspect of the whale—so often identified as the Leviathan of the bible—as a symbol of death, while the positive aspect corresponds to rebirth.

In the pages that follow, we tell the story of cetaceans—from the wholesale slaughter of centuries past to the close encounters of recent years. Today's whale-watching and cetacean research comes by virtue of technological progress which has allowed naturalists to avail themselves of remarkably sophisticated instruments with which to penetrate the mysterious and remote world of these giant mammals. The successors of Rondelet and Belon have also helped by developing synthetic substitutes for whale ivory and whale oil.

The book is divided into four major sections. The first is devoted entirely to the Cetaceans which, for purely commercial reasons, have borne the brunt of humanity's greed and have been almost wiped out (with some populations becoming entirely extinct). The second section is devoted entirely to the killer whale, the largest of the dolphins, rarely hunted but often identified with atrocious ferocity. The third section examines the dolphins proper, over the past millennia protagonists of touching legends, and over the past decades, the innocent victims of senseless slaughter by the modern fishing industry. We also touch on the close relatives of the dolphins—the beluga whale, with its snowy skin, and the narwhal, probable source of the unicorn legend. The volume concludes with an illustrated reference section that serves to document and describe the appearance and behavior of some of the more than seventy species that belong to the order Cetacea.

Southern right whales spend the summers in the cold antarctic waters, while during the winter—which corresponds roughly in the southern hemisphere to the period from June to September—they gather in warmer regions. Among these regions are the southern tip of South Africa, where the mother and her calf at left were photographed, and the Valdés Peninsula in Patagonia, temporary home of the right whale shown above. The right whales come to these winter grounds to mate and to give birth to their young.

PAGES 18–19
The majestic flukes of a diving humpback.

PAGES 20–21
A pair of humpbacks leap in unison.

WHALES AND MAN

Gaetano Cafiero

The Basques who lived on the shores of the Bay of Biscay were the first to unleash the slaughter of whale populations which has yet to cease entirely. Europeans who lived along the Atlantic coast had always been familiar with whales, if only because whales sporadically beached themselves and were found dead or dying. Then, during the reign of Charlemagne, came the first, chance encounter with a live whale—almost certainly a northern right whale—which led the Basque fishermen to begin to wait in ambush off the coast: the whales were slow, meek, and incapable of reacting quickly enough to escape; they could be slaughtered with relative ease. Once they had been killed, the hapless animals remained afloat. Nothing could be simpler for the newly anointed whalers than to tow their prey to shore and cut them into pieces.

In the Middle Ages, the fishing village that later became Biarritz boasted one of the first plants in the world for the processing of whale blubber, flesh, and bones. The Basques invented something they called the *arpoi*—the harpoon—and they gradually began to venture out into the open sea in larger and larger boats driven by ever greater numbers of oarsmen. It is said that the stench rising from the dead whales reached all the way to the shores of England, causing considerable consternation among the fishermen of the British Isles. Considering what happened next, it might be said that the English and Dutch merchants probably sensed, in that unpleasant odor, the air of profit; both nations began to fund the Basques, purchasing all of the oil that could be extracted from their huge victims. The Basques, in turn, worked to improve their methods of hunting, building entire fleets of whaling ships in which they pursued their prey all the way to Iceland and along the coasts of Newfoundland. And it was off the shores of Newfoundland, in what are now Canadian territorial waters, that Basque ships first hailed Icelandic and Viking ships, which carried other seafarers who had already discovered the immensely profitable whale trade.

Those early whalers flourished while exhausting the very resource that made them wealthy, slaughtering an incredible number of whales, wiping out entire populations. Unfortunately, the whales could not learn from the experience. But humans could. And they learned that the ocean was stocked with whales in far greater numbers than the whales they had wiped out.

It is significant that the *Eubalaena glacialis* (if that is indeed the same whale the Basques hunted down in such large numbers) was called the "black right whale" by the

English. The "right" in the name meant simply that this was the best whale to hunt and to kill because it offered the best combination of weight, ease of capture, and yield of oil. However, the hunters would hunt whatever presented itself—the little minke whale, the humpback whale, the bowhead whale, the fin whale, and the sperm whale. Later, in the nineteenth century, they hunted the blue whale, the largest mammal and perhaps the largest animal ever to appear on the face of the earth.

When the English and the Dutch, who already dominated the oceans, decided to set up business as whalers, they did so with considerable zeal. All others, including the Basque pioneers, had to settle back and be satisfied with a secondary role or even take service under the new masters of the open sea. The first to discover the whales of the Arctic Sea was the English captain Jonas Poole, in June of 1583. He was one of the many seafarers sent by Queen Elizabeth in search of the famous Northwest Passage, which was meant to shorten the voyage for trading ships heading to the Orient. Europeans looked to the markets of Asia, seeking out new contacts with China and Japan, which they considered to be countries almost as advanced as their own and certainly very wealthy. Ninety-one years earlier, Christopher Columbus had been entrusted with the same mission—to reach the Far East by sailing west. One year and one month later, the Dutch navigator William Barents discovered an island already well known to the Vikings, that he named Spitsbergen. Barents was just an explorer, however. Little did he imagine that the wonderful place of silent deep bays and glittering glaciers would one day become the world's largest slaughterhouse for whales, that all that immaculate whiteness would be stained with red, and that even the icebergs would one day be crimson with the blood of the whales massacred around them.

Explorations of the Arctic Ocean by the English and Russian mariners served to reassure the venturesome whalers, who had believed until then that the disappearance of black right whales meant the disappearance of all whales. And so began the systematic extermination of the *Balaena mysticetus*, the Greenland whale. Once Europeans had perfected their sailing ships and their navigational techniques, and especially once they had applied the principles of firearms to the harpoon, huge numbers of these playful whales disappeared without a trace. Two centuries later, in the youthful republic of the United States of America, whaling became an industry. Even now, New

FACING
Hunting the Sperm Whale, *an aquatint from 1834, is the only portrayal of a sperm whale by the French artist Garneray, who specialized in portraying the right whale.*

BELOW
An anonymous watercolor, executed around 1880, shows a group of sperm whales trapped in a fjord, probably the Seydisfjord in Iceland. In those days, whalers often hunted cetaceans by driving them into an enclosed bay.

RIGHT
In this oil on canvas, painted in 1617 by the Dutch painter Esaias von den Velde, elegantly dressed spectators observe a beached whale on the sands between Schaveningen and Katwijk.

England is filled with traces of those courageous and tragic years—from the old port of New Bedford, described by Melville in his novel, all the way down to Arrowhead, the town where he wrote the last few chapters—much has remained as it was 150 years ago. On the island of Nantucket, in the Seamen's Bethel, or chapel of the whalers, the cenotaphs on the wall can still bring a lump to the throat of the casual visitor. The Whaling Museum is set in a house that once belonged to a wealthy trader; at the wharf, famed whaling ships such as the *Ladoga*—which could process 100 sperm whales—toss at their moorings.

To a whaler, a whale is a floating goldmine. The blue whale can attain a weight of 130 tons. The spine alone can weigh up to 10 tons, the jaw bone two-and-a-half tons, and the rest of the bones, 23 tons. The musculature alone weighs some 50 tons. From the 25 or so tons of blubber, ten hours of rendering in the boilers of a whaler's "floating factory" could produce 60 or 70 English barrels, each containing about 45 gallons of extremely fine oil. Unlike our ancestors, who found it difficult to resist such abundant bounty, people today have a much broader-based sense of how the environment works and know that many of the same products are available from other, less destructive sources, and, most importantly, that the great cetaceans are an integral part of the marine ecosystem. We further know that the disappearance of these animals could prove to be an enormous loss for humanity.

LEFT
A whaling scene painted on wood by the Japanese artist Nishimura Shigenobu in 1720.

RIGHT
This painting on wood, executed by the Japanese artist Hiroshige, is set in the province of Iki, where watchtowers had been built.

BELOW
This work, attributed to the American artist Charles Sidney Raleigh and completed in 1877, depicts a sperm whale destroying a whale boat with a swat of its tail.

PAGES 28-29
In this 1855 watercolor, the American artist Walter Weir (under the pseudonym Robert Wallace), depicts a spectacular battle between a giant sperm whale and the tiny vessels of the whalers.

HUMPBACK WHALES

I still recall with fondness the morning a splendid humpback whale leapt repeatedly out of a sea swept by strong winds and foamy waves. I was on a course between Jost van Dike in the Virgin Islands, and Cap Haitien in Haiti, setting up some splendid photographs with a 200-mm. lens, aboard the *Alyan*, a 45-foot sloop. I was composing—in the viewfinder of my camera—the spectacular blue of the sky dotted by white and gray clouds, and right in the center of the picture was the striped belly of the whale, huge flippers spread like wings, and clouds of spray across the blue water. I could not get a single shot, however; the sea was too rough, the boat seemed to be racing with the whale and dancing on the foamy surface, and one after another my careful compositions were lost to posterity. I was experiencing a fairly typical form of behavior of this species, the only member of its genus (*Megaptera*, which in Greek means, "great wings"), which despite its massive body is one of the most playful and agile of the baleen whales.

Unlike many other baleen whales, which tend to live in the open sea, the *Megaptera novaeangliae* tends to prefer coastal waters, and it is not uncommon to find it inside harbors or even miles from the open sea in the estuary of a major river. The most spectacular and well known example of this occurred on October 11, 1985, when a humpback (a male, immediately named Humphrey) slipped silently under the huge spans of the Golden Gate Bridge in San Francisco. Humphrey swam across the San Francisco Bay, on beyond Richmond and San Rafael, all the way to San Pablo Bay and on up the Rio Vista until he found his way into the dead-end canal of Shag Slough. It took 25 days of steady work, the assistance of thousands of volunteers, Federal and state police officers, the Navy, the Coast Guard, and an estimated $75,000 to return Humphrey safe and sound to the ocean.

The mating season for the humpback whale is in the winter—February in the northern hemisphere and July-August in the southern hemisphere. Their expressions of affection, the caresses that they exchange, the songs that they sing in the depths of the sea during the mating season are some of the most impressive spectacles that can be observed in nature. When a male and a female float side by side on the surface of the ocean, they exchange blows and smacks with their flippers that are clearly intended as tokens of affection, and which can be heard miles away on clear, calm days. Males and females caress each other with their flippers, roll first in one direction and then in the

other, and leap suddenly out of the water. And they sing. All whales "sing"; although they have no vocal chords, they emit a series of modulated sounds, grunts, roars, whistles, and sighs. That these unique sounds were made by living creatures was only discovered in 1950 in the waters of the Pacific Ocean off the Hawaiian Islands; U.S. Navy counterespionage, suspicious of the underwater concert that at first sounded like the signal of a fleet of enemy submarines (the Korean War was underway), discovered its true source. The studies that were conducted in order to understand the causes of this behavior made it possible to establish that the songs of the humpback whale vary—that is, the sounds produced by the whales of the Caribbean are different from the sounds produced in Australia or in the Marshall Islands. It would appear that only the males sing. And since these singing sessions tend to correspond to the mating season, it is clear that the ulterior motive behind the serenade is far different from that behind the emission of other sounds by the toothed whales, who use these sounds as a type of sonar which allows them to hunt prey at night or in murky water.

The humpback is classified as a member of the family of rorqual whales, the largest members of the suborder, all the way up to the 108 feet in length and the 130 tons of weight of the blue whale. The humpback's flippers can attain a length of close to a third of the body's total length. The physical structure of the rorquals is more streamlined than that of the right whales: the length of their heads is no more than a quarter of the total body length; the head tends to be somewhat flat, with elongated jaws; and their plates of baleen—anywhere between 270 and 400 in number—are far shorter, broader, and stiffer. Their pectoral flippers are thinner and pointed, there is a dorsal fin, the cervical vertebrae are not joined, and the subcutaneous layer of blubber is relatively thin, making these animals fast swimmers.

The most evident features that distinguish the family are the ventral grooves, which can vary in number from 40 to 100 (in the humpback, from 14 to 35), and mark the animal's throat. These folds allow the oral cavity to swell considerably so as to accommodate an enormous quantity of sea water rich in the plankton on which these baleen cetaceans feed. When the whale closes its mouth, the folds reappear and the tongue is compressed against the palate, pushing out the water through the filter formed by the whalebones, or baleens, which capture small fish and crustaceans.

ABOVE AND FACING
Of all the whales, humpbacks possess the most easily identifiable shape, with their large white flippers a third the length of the whale's entire body. Humpbacks, like all rorqual whales, have the distinctive ventral grooves along the length of their bellies. These folds expand, allowing the animal to feed by ingesting huge quantities of plankton-rich water. Humpbacks are generally found in groups of two or three; only in rare cases do they form small schools of a dozen or so. The fact that they make use of complex sounds leads scientists to think that they may communicate with each other over vast distances.

Humpback whales are present in all the oceans, but they tend to stay near the polar icecaps. In schools of four to twelve whales, they make long migrations, constantly in search of cold waters where the krill and huge schools of sardines, anchovies, and cod on which they feed are bountiful. These whales, then, are found in polar waters in the summer and tropical waters in the winter, their huge black bodies (only the throat and the tips of the huge pectoral flippers are white) ripped by deep cuts, stripes, shark bites, and the sores caused by barnacles.

The fact that humpback whales tend to prefer coastal waters has made it possible to perform relatively advanced studies on these animals; there are now spectacular films and photographic studies. Nevertheless, no one has ever succeeded in documenting the actual mating process. The most in-depth research has been conducted along the coasts of the Hawaiian Islands and the West Indies. Here, during the fifties, as we have already stated, the songs of the whales were recorded for the first time, and only during more recent times have they been analyzed and explained. It has been possible to establish that humpbacks rarely sing while feeding or when moving along their migratory routes. In general, it is solitary adult males who make use of the songs to court females or else to ward off their rivals, just as do a great many species of birds. Mating and births take place on an average every two or three years, and the mating season constitutes an extremely important social event in the lives of these cetaceans. Gatherings of males have been observed clustering around a single female whale, thrusting and beating each other with their flippers and lashing out with their tails to win the best and closest position to the prospective mate. The males attempt to daunt each other by swelling their throats so as to appear larger and intimidate their competitors. Other aggressive signals that are typical of the male humpback are swimming rapidly with the head held erect out of the water, the act of smacking the surface of the ocean with the tail, beating the pectoral flippers one against the other, and trailing a line of bubbles from the blowhole while under water, presumably to confuse their adversaries. Combat between male humpbacks can leave clearly visible marks on the bodies of the defeated whales—bruises, deep cuts, and bloody wounds that attract sharks and killer whales.

In this regard, a remarkable form of behavior has been observed among killer whales—they tend to attack humpbacks with little bites, ripping away small strips of

FACING, UPPER
Two humpback whales swim in the cold waters of the Antarctic Ocean; the whale populations that converge on this region in the summer come from South America, Africa, Australia, and New Zealand.

FACING, LOWER
Although much of the world population of humpbacks has been decimated by the large-scale whaling of the past, they still can be found in every sea in the world. They abound in the icy waters of Antarctica as well as the tropical waters of the West Indies. A group that has been studied extensively is the humpbacks that spend their summers in Glacier Bay, Alaska, where the whales are often sighted a few dozen yards off-shore. The humpbacks of the southern hemisphere spend their feeding season in the Antarctic seas. It is believed that the populations of the two hemispheres seldom, if ever, mingle.

flesh and chunks of meat from the living cetaceans, and only once they have singled out the weakest humpback, fatigued and damaged in the battles with other male humpbacks, do they attack this individual en masse, killing and devouring it.

Humpbacks are well known for their great leaps out of the water, for which a number of interpretations have been offered: aggression, inspection of the surrounding environment, long-distance communication. They are also often observed waving a pectoral flipper in the air as they float on the surface rolled over on one side; this may be yet another expression of aggression, or sign of determination to defend a territory, but it is most hauntingly interpreted as a form of salutation to other whales or to humans who have drawn too close.

Humpback behavior changes entirely when the animals reach their summer pastures. The whales gather in groups of a dozen or so. These groups are fairly unstable; the animals scatter, hook up with other schools, and then return to the original group. Only the females with their young form stable groups. The size of the group seems to be correlated to the size of the shoal of fish or colony of crustaceans that form the chief source of food; perhaps this behavior of reciprocal friendship serves to better coordinate the activities of the group so that all the whales can enjoy a greater abundance of food. Other opportunities for assembly and cooperation are infrequent—it has been observed that couples of whales might travel together for a day, at best, along a migratory route; the day after, the whales swim off independently, perhaps to meet again at a later occasion, perhaps offered by a particularly rich feeding ground. All of this would suggest that humpback society calls for mating in a sort of harem without constraints of time or space, in which only a few males manage to impregnate the female in heat. Concerning the actual function and significance of the whales' songs—as complex and elaborate as their combat—only conjectures can be made. We do not know why the rhythms, refrains, and "lyrics" of the songs change continually, or why different populations of humpbacks sing in different ways.

We also know very little about the dangers these whales face from sharks and killer whales. We have documentation of unsuccessful attacks by packs of killer whales upon couples of humpbacks accompanying a young whale, and large sharks have been seen apparently stalking the whales, but we do not know whether a lurking shark will attack its cetacean prey. It is, on the other hand, quite

The pectoral fins of the humpback whale, typically knobby along the edges, are infested with parasites, as are other parts of the body, such as the head. In the cold waters, a single animal can carry as much as a half ton of parasites, especially barnacles and other small sessile crustaceans similar to those found on shoals and reefs. When humpbacks migrate toward warmer regions, some of *the barnacles are lost and replaced by another crustacean, the* Cyamus boopis, *a parasite that "specializes" in humpbacks. In these photographs, the humpbacks are shown roughly clapping their pectoral fins against the surface of the sea, as they often do, making a sound quite similar to a gunshot. This seems to be a form of communication, but scientists are not yet sure of its exact meaning.*

In the summer, humpbacks migrate toward the cold waters of the poles in order to take advantage of the great abundance of food available there. In the northern hemisphere, they feed for the most part on such small fish as herring, mackerel, and anchovies. In the waters of the Antarctic, they tend to filter mostly the small shrimplike crustaceans called krill. These photographs show a humpback feeding. First, it takes a mouthful of water and food (above). As soon as the mouth closes (top right), the water is expelled from the sides and the baleen hanging from the palate (visible in the photograph at right) retains everything that is edible. Seagulls, always ready to take advantage of every situation, try to take part in the banquet.

Of all baleen whales, the ones that leap out of the water most frequently are the humpbacks. The typical leap includes a sort of twirl around the longitudinal axis of the whale's body. It is not known just what drives the big cetaceans to make these spectacular leaps, but a number of hypotheses have been advanced. In the opinion of some, humpbacks leap out of the water in order to rid themselves of skin parasites; others think that it is nothing more than play, a way of taking a look around, or of communicating. Some believe that the leaping could be a way of sending a threatening sign to boats that draw too close; most researchers and other visitors, however, say that they have not had the impression that the humpback was sending any menacing signs in their direction.

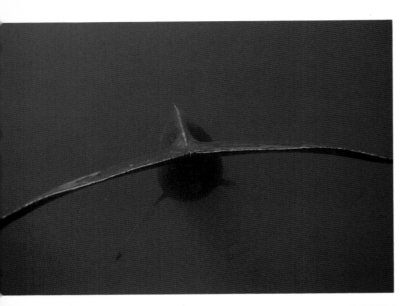

ABOVE

Many of the underwater photographs of humpbacks are taken in Hawaii, where the water is particularly clear and where many of the animals spend the winter, either mating or giving birth to the young conceived during the previous year.

well known that whalers have been successful in the past in recruiting killer whales to collaborate in the hunting of humpbacks. With the assistance of killer whales, whalers have managed to slaughter great numbers of humpbacks that, when frightened by the onslaught of the killer whales, retreated into sheltered bays.

Humans learned quickly how to develop more effective systems of whaling, but we are less adept at developing systems of research into the way of life of whales, at overcoming environmental barriers to the identification of individuals, and at understanding how toothed whales use their natural instruments of echolocation. We are also historically more adept at hunting than at using satellite and radio telemetry to establish the migratory routes of whales, and at gathering physiological data and DNA "fingerprints" in order to establish the relations between the individuals of a single species and to improve our knowledge of the reproductive patterns of marine animals.

The humpback's size and the extensive migrations it performs, from the tropics to the poles, halfway across the planet, makes it a sort of microcosm on which other animals (such as cirriped crustaceans) live. These barnacles, which spend their lives hidden in their calcareous shells solidly attached to reefs and shoals, have found an ideal habitat on the skin of the humpback whale. The whale emerges to breathe, and it is like a reef at low tide; the whale dives deep, and the tiny crustaceans begin breathing underwater, absorbing the tiny particles on which they feed. In turn, the cirripeds—often Coronulae—with their hard white shells, serve as a solid substrate for colonies of yet another parasite, the conchoderma. In the skin of the humpbacks this sea worm finds an ideal surrogate for the floating pieces of wood that it usually attaches itself to. Both these families of parasites gradually depart from the humpback's body as the summer season progresses and the water becomes warmer. An individual humpback may host a mass of almost a half ton of parasites, bearing them through the seas of the world until their life cycles end.

The relationship between humpbacks and the *Pseudorca crassidens*, or false killer whale, remains a mystery. Dr. Sylvia A. Earle, a celebrated American naturalist who studies marine animals in their environment, once observed a huge assembly of humpback whales and false killer whales in the Hawaiian Islands. It may have simply been a freak event rather than a significant observation, but an explanation has yet to be found.

FACING

In the winter quarters of the humpback, it is possible to listen to their long and sonorous songs. These might be the songs that ancient mariners claimed to have heard, thinking them to be mermaids or sirens; indeed, at times, the sounds of the humpbacks can be heard through the hull of a ship. Today, researchers study them with the assistance of hydrophones; nonetheless, their true meaning is in part unknown. We do know that it is the males that sing, and that probably this singing has some role in courtship or sexual competition. Often, while singing, the whales hang motionless in the water, as in this photograph.

Off the Hawaiian Islands, the young of the humpbacks are born in January; in the Caribbean, they are born between January and February. The newborn whale never leaves its mother's side, depending on her for protection from predators and for nourishment—the milk is extremely rich in fats. Mother and calf will spend at least a year together, until the young whale is weaned during the following winter. Only then will the mother whale be able to mate once again. This rule applies, in general, to other species of cetaceans. The consequence is that each female will bear offspring at most every two years. For this reason, the populations of dolphins and whales increase very slowly and are extremely vulnerable to decimation through hunting.

Often, humpback whales tranquilly allow boats and scuba divers to approach them, and they even seem curious about their visitors. Researchers have discovered, however, that these whales can be annoyed by the air bubbles released by a scuba diver. This female with a young whale seems to be eyeing the photographer with a mixture of curiosity and apprehension.

Although all cetaceans have adapted surprisingly well to the underwater environment, they are still dependent on the surface, where they must return periodically to breathe. In this photograph, a humpback dives after "blowing."

This small group is not, as it might seem, a family group. Indeed, among humpbacks, as among most types of whales, the bond between the sexes ends after copulation, and so the second adult may well not be the father of the young whale. It could be another female or a new suitor intent on testing the availability of the new mother.

PAGES 48–49
A humpback photographed off Hawaii, accompanied by a group of melon-headed whales (one of the many species in the family Delphinidae).

GRAY WHALES

In an intermediate position between rorqual whales and right whales and not closely related to either of these two groups, the gray whale has been placed by naturalists in a family all its own. The family is the Eschrichtiidae, and the gray whale is the *Eschrichtius robustus*. It is a cetacean of medium size, no longer than 50 feet, with a relatively small head. On either side of the mouth it possesses between 138 and 174 plates of baleen, rather large and long, up to a foot and a half. The gray whale's neck is marked by two to four ventral grooves, with sparse hairs on the jaw. The pectoral fins are of medium length. The gray whale tends to live along the coasts. Recent observations have shown that gray whales often swim extremely close to the beach and wallow around in just two-and-a-half feet of water, grazing on the sandy floor, eating annelids, polychaetes, gastropods, and crustaceans while waiting for high tide. Often found in the northern Pacific Ocean, the gray whale will swim as far south as the California coast between November and May. For over eighty years, from 1851 until 1937, the gray whale was hunted and killed indiscriminately. In 1851, during the season of migration, from mid-December until the end of January, one could count more than 1,000 whales a day off the California coasts. Just 23 years later, there were about 40 a day, and after another 30 years, in the first decade of this century, the gray whale was considered to be extinct. Then, a few gray whales were sighted off the Siberian and Alaskan coasts, and in the winter of 1925-1926, 42 of the whales that had reappeared in the waters off California were slaughtered. Finally, in 1937, when the world population of gray whales may have dropped to just 250 (the claim was made, though never proved), they were put off limits to whalers. Thirty years later, 18,300 gray whales were counted in a survey.

FACING, UPPER
In the lagoons along the Pacific coast of Baja, California, large groups of gray whales gather each year. These animals, which have been a protected species for decades, allow visitors and photographers to approach them.

FACING, LOWER
The yellowish spots that appear on the skin of the gray whales are small crustaceans. Many cetaceans are infested with such parasites, some of which are specialized to particular cetacean species. As far as we know, the parasites do not cause their hosts much trouble or annoyance, nor do they cause much physical harm, even though when they finally release from the whale's skin, in warmer waters, they do leave permanent scars.

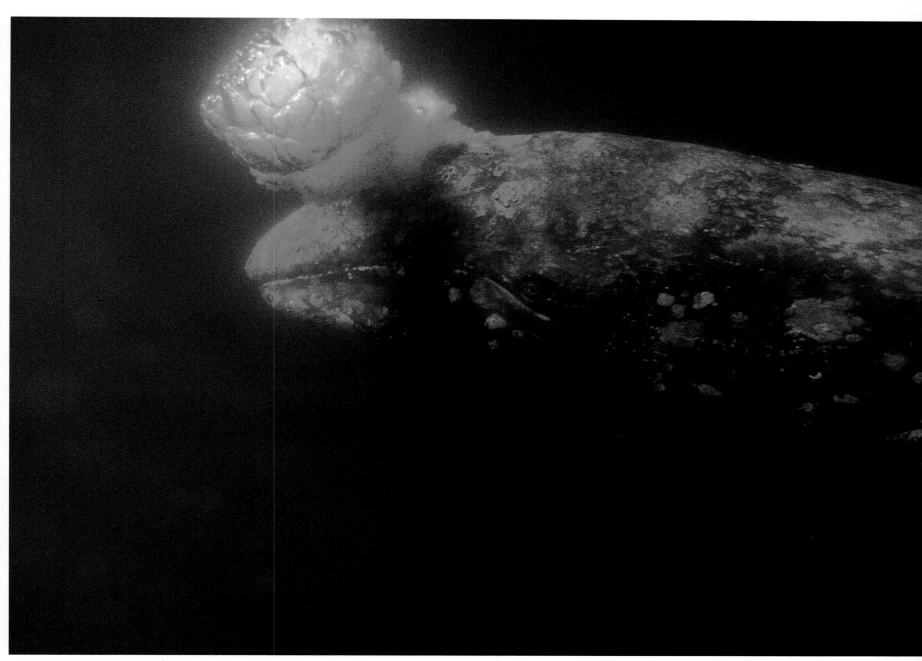

FACING

This gray whale obligingly opened its mouth for the photographer, revealing its tongue and plates of baleen. In the photograph above, a gray whale releases large air bubbles from its blowhole while still underwater. This behavior is thought to signal annoyance.

PAGES 54–55

A gray whale surfaces amid a vast expanse of kelp, the giant seaweed found along the coasts of California.

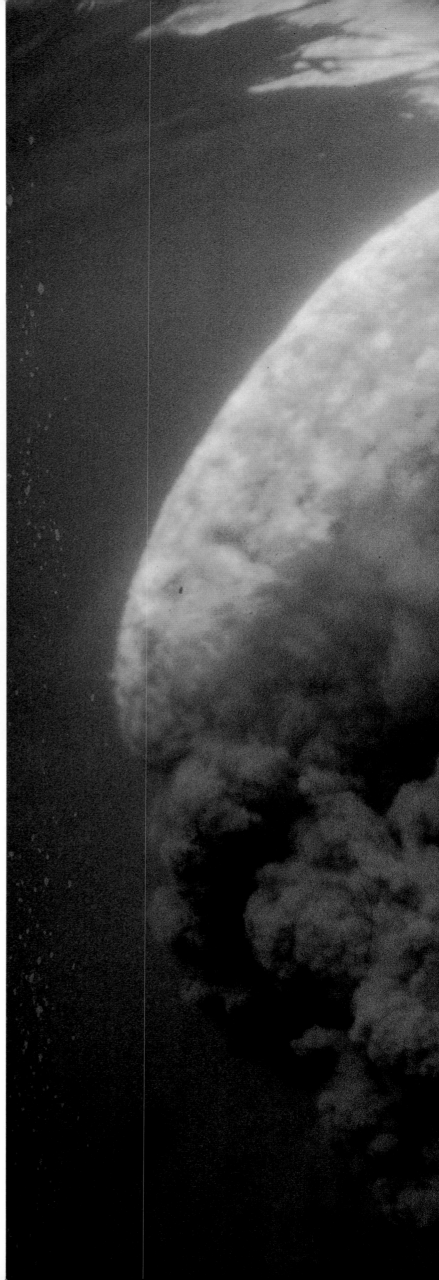

Gray whales obtain nourishment in a remarkable manner, differently from almost all other baleen whales. Rather than searching for plankton floating in the water, they hunt and eat animals that live on the seabed. Their technique involves rolling over on one side and then swimming slowly along, their mouths just grazing the sea floor, sucking in mud and food—small shrimp, crustaceans, polychaetes, and mollusks. When they feed, the gray whales dig great trenches as they go, literally plowing the sea floor, which indirectly serves to increase the productivity of the zone. One of the areas in which this feeding behavior has been studied is on the Pacific Coast, just off Vancouver, Canada.

RIGHT WHALES

FACING, UPPER

A diving right whale. For the most part, this species does not descend to very great depths, in part because the plankton on which they feed is generally found on the surface. Right whales can remain underwater without breathing for about 20 minutes.

FACING, LOWER

Right whales obtain nourishment by filtering plankton on the surface of the sea; to do this they swim slowly with their mouths open while moving through the areas most heavily populated with floating life forms. The animal's mouth is one huge filter—the head of a right constitutes as much as a third of its entire body length. The baleen plates are six to ten feet long and are folded away in the oral cavity; in order to make room for them, the bones of the upper part of the mouth are typically arched upwards.

The luck of the southern right whale (*Eubalaena australis*) was not much better than that of the gray whale. This whale lived and traveled in great schools in the coastal waters off Argentina, South Georgia, South Africa, Australia, and New Zealand. This was basically the southern counterpart of the *Eubalaena glacialis*, the black right whale that the Basques had hunted so long ago. Indeed, the English whalers dubbed this whale the southern right whale— and the "right" meant that this was the right whale to kill, in terms of the quantity and quality of the oil, in the southern hemisphere. Without a doubt, the scientific name (*eu-* is a Greek prefix meaning "good," or "well," while *australis* is Latin for "southern") was developed only after the whalers themselves had given the whale this explicit and pragmatic name.

Scientists have not yet developed a clear classification of the right whales, and it is not yet known whether there are one, two, or three separate species. There is no clear external morphological basis for distinguishing the southern right whales from their northern relatives. Like the northern right whale, the southern has a stocky body, an average of 50 feet in length, and a maximum of 60 feet. The thick skin is marked with calluses above the eyes and on the mandible and jaw; in these calluses live colonies of whale lice. From these areas of the whale's body it is possible to detect minor physical distinctions—the callus on the lower lip is slightly more substantial in the southern whale than in its northern cousin. Skin color is a pale dirty gray at birth and darkens gradually during growth until it becomes an intense black at adulthood, with white spots, especially in the ventral area.

The southern right whale is very slowly recovering from the intense exploitation to which it was subjected in the past. The slowness of the species' recovery leads scientists to hypothesize that this whale's rate of reproduction is rather low, and that its rate of mortality, conversely, is rather high. It would seem that the tropical waters between 20 degrees north and 20 degrees south are an insurmountable barrier, keeping the southern right whales from intruding on the territory of their northern counterparts and vice versa. The southern right whale has found a safe haven along the coast of the Valdés peninsula in Argentina, and the northern in the Bay of Fundy in Canada, where hundreds of the animals gather to mate and to bear their young, which are up to 20 feet long.

BELOW

In the southern hemisphere, the calves of the southern right whale, about 18 feet long at birth, are born between July and November. In their wintering grounds, veritable nurseries can develop, in which the females and the young are left on their own.

BELOW AND RIGHT

Two closeups of right whales, taken in the waters around the Valdés Peninsula in Argentina. It is in this gathering area, discovered in 1969, that much of the research done on right whales has been accomplished.

PAGES 62–63
Undoubtedly curious about his observer, a southern right whale displays no signs of fear or annoyance and allows a scuba diver to approach and take photographs. An adult can measure from 50 to 60 feet in length.

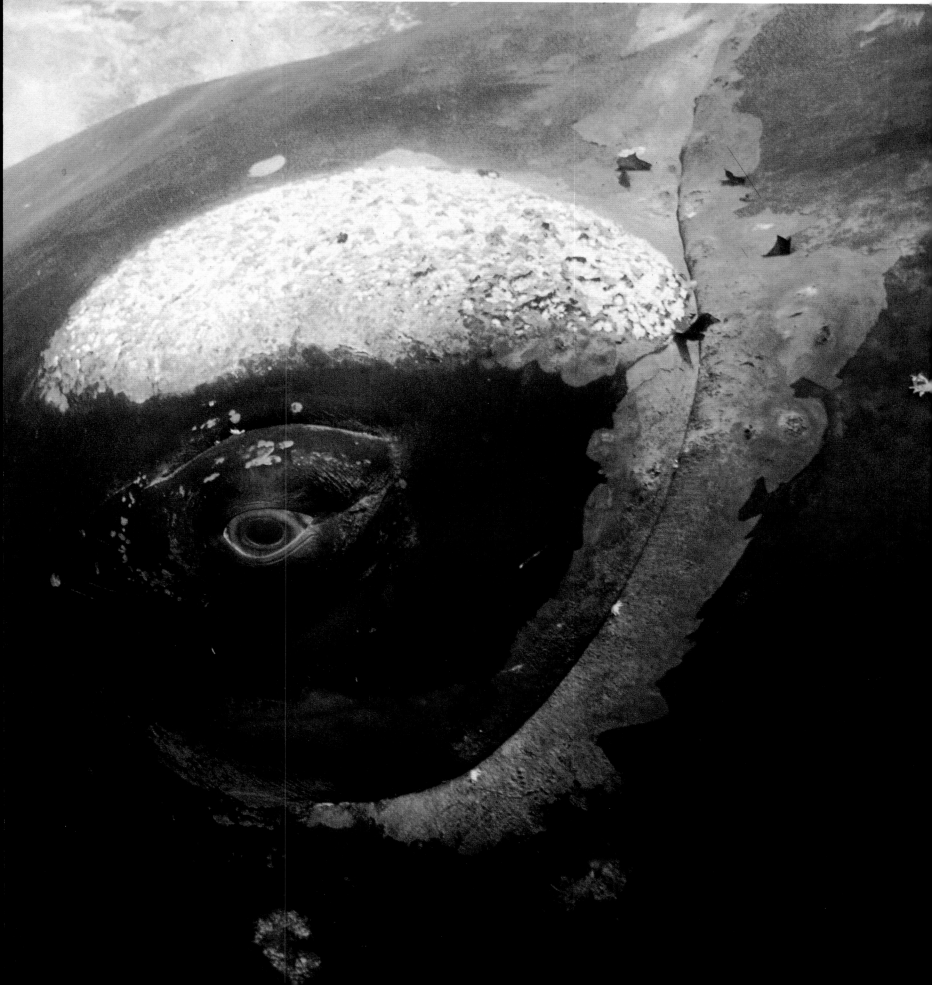

BLUE WHALES
AND FIN WHALES

Whales are the largest living animals; the underlying reasons have to do with the laws of physics and with certain consequential evolutionary adaptations. As the body size of an animal increases, both the overall weight and the strength of the skeleton and power of the musculature increase exponentially. However, the weight increases cubically, while the skeleton and musculature increase quadratically (by cubes as opposed to squares); this is because the bones and muscles vary only according to the cross-section of the body and not its length. Therefore, when an animal reaches a length that is double its length at birth, its weight has increased eightfold, while the power of its muscles and the strength of its bones have increased only four-fold.

This means that a land animal cannot exceed certain limits in its body size. It has been calculated that the Brontosaurus weighed about a quarter of what the blue whale weighs. In water, it is buoyancy, not musculature, that supports the weight of a whale. The largest living animal (and one must suppose, the largest animal ever to exist) is the blue whale. Before the species was horribly decimated by whalers in the last century, individuals were measured at over 98 feet in length, weighing something like 160 tons. Such easy bounty could hardly fail to attract human greed—hunting blue whales was sharply restricted in the southern hemisphere in the early sixties, and abolished entirely around the world in 1965, but in the meantime the blue whales to be found in the Pacific Ocean had dwindled to just over 1,000, and perhaps a few hundred were left in the waters of the North Atlantic. Of the more than 200,000 blue whales scattered through the oceans of the southern hemisphere in the nineteenth century, there were fewer than 10,000 by the end of this century, and half of those were pygmy blue whales.

The fin whale, named for its dorsal fin, which is more pronounced and evident than that of other baleen whales, closely resembles the blue whale. Indeed, in terms of size—a maximum length of 80 feet in northern waters and nearly 90 feet in southern waters—it does not differ greatly from its bluish relative. It does have some significant differences, however. Most notably, despite its size, the fin whale is one of the fastest whales. It generally moves at a velocity ranging from 2 to 8 knots, it is capable of sprinting at more than 17 knots—more than 20 miles per hour.

Left

The second largest animal on earth, immediately after the blue whale, is the fin whale. It can be recognized by its jaw which, unlike the blue whale's, is white. Still more peculiar, however, is the fact that this coloration is asymmetrical— only the right mandible is white, while the left is slate grey like the rest of the body. It is believed this peculiarity is useful in feeding; when the fin whale eats, it often turns on its side with the right side facing downward, and in this position the lighter coloration of the head makes it less visible to the intended prey beneath.

Right

Two views of another member of the rorqual family of baleen whales, the minke whale. This is the smallest species in the family—at its largest it measures about 35 feet in length. Today, these whales are the most frequently hunted members of the family, mainly in Antarctica. After decimating the populations of the larger species, the last industrial whaling nations, such as Japan, have nothing left but to hunt down the smaller animals, which are still relatively numerous. Now there is a danger that these small rorquals will face the same fate as the giant blue whales.

A fin whale feeds on the surface; the setting sun lights the back of the mouth, which appears pink. The whale's ventral grooves expand in order to accommodate the water, and one can see the baleen protruding from the jaw. In rorqual whales, the whalebones are stiff and fairly short (they are no longer than 30 inches); the ends splay into a great many smaller strips, forming a sort of enormous brush.

SPERM WHALES

The ship was slicing through the water, fast and graceful. The *Orca* in those years—the early seventies—was a splendid vessel. She was 50 feet long overall, sloop-rigged, with a flush deck, and without the bulk of a deckhouse, always an obstacle to rapid handling. The breeze was light and the sea was calm and transparent. We were on a heading for Arbatax, in Sardinia. We had cast off from a dock in the port of Fiumicino, and had run under power for only a few minutes, just at first, to get underway and clear of the boats double- and triple-moored and then to get clear of the breakwater, a diabolical trap for cabin sailboats. In the distance, invisible in the green water, there was a slight wave accumulation of sandy water, an underwater dune, where the waters of the Tiber flowed into the waters of the Mediterranean Sea. There we saw the deep-sea-fishing boats returning to port, engines gunning full force so as to avoid smashing into the breakwater, losing their ponderous cargo, and perhaps sinking the boat in the bargain. The fishing boats raised a wake of their own, making life harder for boats under sail, as we were. We had made good headway and sailed half of our charted route, 165 miles at 227 degrees. We were smack in the middle of the Tyrrhenian Sea on a beautiful mid-summer day, and it looked like we were in the Antilles. The *Orca* cut through the water with a hiss. Suddenly, both Vito—skipper and owner of the *Orca*—and I saw it at the same time, a dark silhouette, shapely and clean, moving along at the same speed as we were, as if it were a shadow cast by the boat itself. We were slightly concerned. Vito and I tried to piece this mystery together, our throats tight with apprehension, our minds crowded with ancient apparitions. The form emerged from the shadows, for a moment it wavered and faded in the blinding glare of the sun's rays reflected from the sea's surface, and then it took shape, gave signs of life, emitted a blast of spray slightly to one side, and our doubts were gone—it was a sperm whale, serving as our escort. It was just a bit longer than the *Orca*'s 50 feet, and we could not even guess at its intentions. Not that a cetacean can have what we would call intentions, of course, even though there is a huge brain tucked away in its massive cranium.

In any case, finding oneself sailing along in the company of a beast of that size is an experience one does not soon forget. Even if our sperm whale was black and not white, we thought back to the final battle of the *Pequod* against Moby Dick, and to the corpse of Captain Ahab tangled in the lines of the harpoons rammed into the back of the immortal whale, finally dragged down into the

depths, bearing all his curses with him. An encounter with a sperm whale in the Tyrrhenian is not a common event; nor is it entirely unheard of. A long time after that sighting of ours, in 1981, three fellow scuba divers from Palermo, members of GRO Sub—Alberto Romeo, a physician and noted underwater photographer, his wife Lucia Scordato, and Piero Di Gregorio—encountered one in the waters off the Aeolian Islands. This sperm whale had run into some trouble and was in poor condition. The sperm whale had encountered one of the notorious southern Italian *spadare*, or fishing trawlers, its nets drifting behind it for miles, designed to catch swordfish but also a deadly trap for dolphins and other protected species. The mesh and the cables of the nets had become tangled around the poor creature's jaw and its immense tail and had cut deeply into the flesh, ripping deep gouges into the back, the belly, and the fins. The sperm whale had come to the surface caught in this giant straitjacket. The three divers leapt into the water with masks, flippers, and camera, and while they were photographing away, other friends and colleagues were working with knives, hacking away at the bonds that confined the promethean beast. It was a long and delicate task performed with considerable trepidation, out of fear that some inadvertent gesture, a cut made accidentally in the body of the trapped and wounded giant, could trigger a furious reaction. But the whale seemed to understand, and it floated calmly, allowing the frenetic humans to rip, cut away, and unravel the terrible netting. Only when it finally felt that it was free did it dive deep into the sea.

ABOVE AND FACING
Sperm whales diving and surfacing. Sperm whales spend remarkably long periods under water, remaining submerged for more than two hours without breathing; they feed on giant squid, which live at extreme depths. When they return to the surface to breathe, the great cetaceans show their characteristic surfacing profile—a small fin (actually a sort of hump) with an indistinct shape and a series of knobs. The blow is quite unusual. At sea it is possible to recognize a sperm whale by its blow alone: it is low and asymmetrical, and always directed off to the left and forward.

PAGES 72-73
Sperm whales belong to the suborder of the toothed whales; that is to say they have teeth instead of baleen and thus are considered to be closer relatives to dolphins than to baleen whales. In this picture it is possible to see the sperm whale's distinctive peglike teeth.

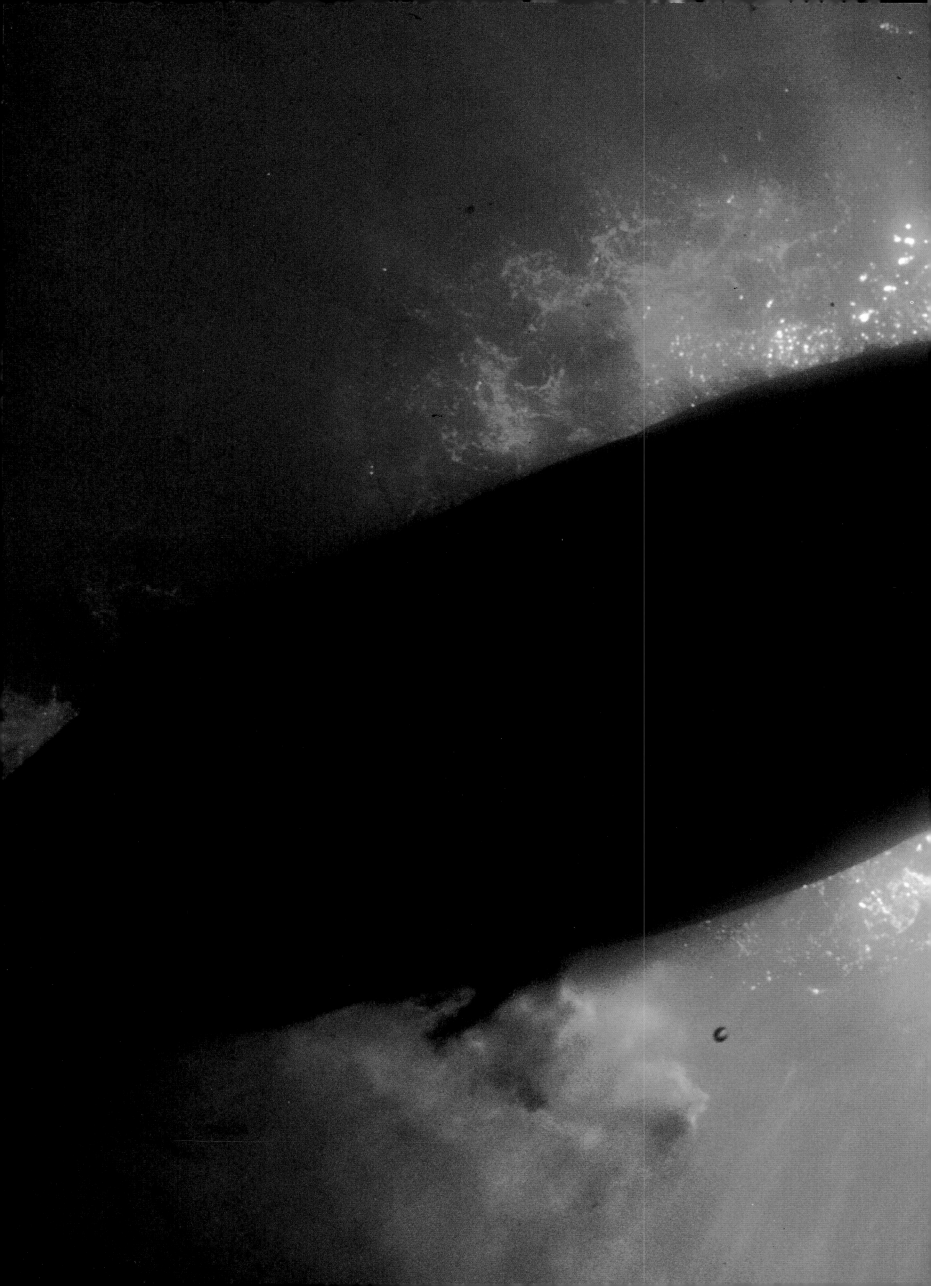

The most famous of the monsters that tormented the sleep of sailors was Leviathan—mentioned often in the bible. The tendency to identify Leviathan as a sperm whale was validated in Herman Melville's *Moby Dick*. Squid—including giant squid, at times longer than the sperm whale itself—constitute the daily fare of this toothed whale. Sperm whales have long been hunted for the enormous amount of oil—up to several hundred gallons—found in the huge head (easily a third of the average fifty-foot length of the body, hence the original scientific name, *Physeter macrocephalus*, which in Greek means "big-headed typhoon," though nowadays the more widely accepted scientific name is *Physeter catodon*). This oil was once believed to be seminal fluid, and it earned the *Physeter catodon* its English name. The Italian name—*capodoglio*, "oil head,"—is far more accurate. There is also the ambergris that can be extracted from the whale's intestine. It would appear that this is the remains of imperfectly digested beaks from the cephalopods the whale feeds on. To obtain squid, the sperm whale can dive to well over 6,500 feet deep. The sperm whale is capable of longer and deeper dives than any other marine mammal.

The diet of the sperm whale is the cause of the beast's occasionally being found drowned on the ocean floor, its lower jaw locked irretrievably onto an underwater telephone cable it probably mistook for the tentacles of a giant squid. The injuries found on the bodies of sperm whales, clearly produced by the powerful jaws and the suckers on the tentacles of squid, would indicate that the squid defend themselves furiously against the attacks of sperm whales, and not—as some have supposed—that the squid attack the sperm whales in order to feed on them. But in the case of giant squid, which can be some 30 feet longer than sperm whales, stories have been handed down about prey becoming predator—squid attacking whale.

Herman Melville described the scene persuasively:

"A vast, pulpy mass, furlongs in length and breadth, of a glancing cream-color, lay floating on the water, innumerable long arms radiating from its center, and curling and twisting like a nest of anacondas, as if blindly to clutch at any hapless object within reach. No perceptible face or front did it have; no conceivable token of either sensation or instinct; but undulated there on the billows, an unearthly, formless, chance-like apparition of life.

"As with a low sucking sound it slowly disappeared again, Starbuck, still gazing at the agitated waters where it had sunk, with a wild noise exclaimed—'Almost rather had I seen Moby Dick and fought him, than to have seen thee, thou white ghost!'

"'What was it, sir?' said Flask.

"'The great live squid, which, they say, few whale ships ever beheld, and returned to their ports to tell of it.'

"But Ahab said nothing; turning his boat, he sailed back to the vessel; the rest as silently following."

In the nineteenth century, the pastures of the southern oceans were very rich, and the ships that set sail from the north Atlantic to brave the seas beyond South Africa's Cape of Good Hope or Cape Horn at the far tip of South America were ever more numerous. According to the Whale Chart—the map of cetacean populations issued in 1851 by the U.S. Navy oceanographer Matthew Maury—there was a remarkably dense whale population in the southern seas, especially in the Pacific Ocean. This was the setting in which Herman Melville placed *Moby Dick*. Here the winds follow a rigid cyclonic structure and can shift in the space of a few minutes from pleasant breezes to shrieking tempests, with gusts at 100 knots and waves 50 feet tall. Because of the wind, it is so cold even in summer that the sheets on the bunks of the old, unheated ships often froze stiff as boards. The same thing would happen to the rigging; it would freeze solid and be broken free only at the cost of nightmarish struggles by men with reddened hands who could breathe only by turning their backs to the wind. The ships would roll so sharply that the yardarms of the square sails would dip into the water.

The blowhole of the sperm whale is not located at the center of the head, as it is in all other toothed whales, but is shifted slightly to the left. This is why the blow is slightly asymmetrical. The shape of the head, too, is slightly peculiar. High and squared off in profile, but rather narrow at the sides, it accounts for 30 percent of the animal's length and contains the so-called "organ of spermaceti," full of a waxy substance that was once believed, erroneously, to be sperm. To this day, we do not know the real function of this substance, but one of the many theories advanced is that it serves to balance the buoyant force during dives. There was a time when the spermaceti was the most valuable trophy for a whaler, along with ambergris, used in perfumery. Ambergris is a remarkable substance found in large chunks, weighing up to 225 pounds, in the intestines of sperm whales. It seems to form around residual, undigested bits of food.

KILLER WHALES

The killer whale's English name, with its gory associations, finds equivalents in most other languages. This fascinating creature has been transformed into a blood-thirsty monster, a sort of mammalian shark. For that matter, in the collective imagination, in pop mythology, in literature, and in film, cetaceans and sharks are not clearly separated into categories as they are in nature. In actuality, the killer whale is nothing more than an oversized dolphin. Like the dolphin, and like the sperm whale, it is a cetacean with teeth. But the dolphin feeds on fish, and the sperm whale lives on squid—both of which are silent prey, captured and consumed under water. The killer whale eats fish too, but it also preys on animals such as seals and penguins. In order to obtain its prey, the killer whale will go so far as to break holes through slabs of ice so that wingless arctic birds and seals fall through. At other times the killer whale will leap onto the beaches crowded with both avian and mammalian prey, savaging the young and stragglers with spectacular lunges. This predatory behavior has captured the imagination of onlookers and has earned the animal its intimidating name.

There is only one species of killer whale, divided geographically into a number of populations, further broken down into schools that claim a given territory; each of these schools has its own structure and physiognomy, perhaps not unlike the ancient human tribal system. It has not yet been fully proven, but it is believed that there are reproductive exchanges between the various killer whale populations, and this is one of the reasons that killer whales all resemble one another so closely, with no great variations between those found in the arctic seas and those found in antarctic seas.

Killer whales move through the water with the aid of three types of fins: a caudal fin, a dorsal fin, and two pectoral fins, or flippers. The pectoral flippers are highly developed and allow the killer whale the rapidity of movement required in order to prey on other animals that are just as agile and quick. They also endow the killer whale with an ability not often found in other cetaceans—that of scooting backwards, which is particularly useful when the killer whale wishes, for instance, to tear a jawful of flesh from the side of a whale, or slide back into the sea with a penguin or a seal it has captured on the ice or on the beach. The caudal fin, or fluke, as in all other cetaceans, is horizontal to body, and produces forward thrust by being moved up and down repeatedly. The dorsal fin is a characteristic peculiar to the killer whale. In general, it serves as a

The killer whale is found throughout the world—sightings have been made in tropical regions and in very chilly seas, like those off the Antarctic Peninsula (the photograph shown to the left was taken in Paradise Bay), where their movements seem to be conditioned more by the formation of ice than by the availability of food, as is the case elsewhere. Killer whales belong to the family of the Delphinidae, and are thus nothing more than large black-and-white dolphins. An adult male can measure as much as 30 feet in length and can weigh up to 8 tons; the females are about 23 feet in length and weigh 4 tons.

hydrodynamic stabilizer, and the bigger it is, the faster the killer whale can swim. It is also a secondary sexual attribute, and indeed the dominant male (there is one in each school, even though killer whales are organized into a "matriarchal society") has a taller and more spectacular dorsal fin than the other males.

The killer whale, therefore, would seem to be the only marine mammal that is suitably equipped to be a savage enemy of humanity—its size, its adeptness at leaping (it can shoot as far as 16 feet out of the water), its speed (it can swim at 25 knots) are all factors that could make this cetacean more dangerous to humans than the dreaded shark. There are, however, no confirmed reports that a killer whale has ever attacked—much less killed and devoured—a human being. Certainly, shipwrecked sailors have claimed that their boats were capsized or rammed by killer whales. In the polar regions, tales are common of Eskimos falling victim to killer whales, and in at least one well-documented case, human remains were found in the belly of one, but there is no proof that the human was killed by the whale.

The killer whale can be found in all of the oceans of the world, from the far north to the extreme south; it is quite capable of tolerating heat, but it shows a certain preference for colder waters; this may well be because its preferred prey—whales, penguins and other birds, seals and sea lions—often live in cold water. Ironically, the killer whale's preference for polar seas results in one of the leading causes of fatalities among these cetaceans—shifting ice. Like so many other cetaceans, killer whales can find themselves cut off from the open sea, hemmed in by vast sheets of ice. Just 21 minutes under water—the longest period these cetaceans have been observed to remain without surfacing—is often not enough to reach freedom by swimming under the ice to find an opening. When caught in these icepacks, they often suffocate or, if they do not attempt to swim out, simply die of hunger.

Their fame as predators dates back thousands of years. Pliny, in his *Historia Naturalis*, mentioned an attack by killer whales on other whales in the breeding grounds off Cadiz, Spain. Since then, as humanity's capacity and opportunities for observation have improved, numerous attacks have been described and documented. Among the most dramatic tales are those of giant blue whales surrounded by packs of killer whales like oxen surrounded by wolves, then torn to bits and literally eaten alive. Killer

Among killer whales, the females and the young have a dorsal fin with a shape and proportions quite similar to that of the other members of the dolphin family; among the adult males, the dorsal fin grows very differently, becoming a triangle nearly six feet tall. Killer whales live in well-established family groups, the makeup of which changes only with the birth or death of the members. These stable groups, called pods, may include up to a few dozen individuals. In some cases, schools of more than a hundred killer whales have been observed, but these are always temporary aggregations of a number of different families. The killer whales make use of a broad range of vocalizations, and each family has its own "dialect" which experts are now able to recognize and distinguish. A number of killer whales held in captivity have been categorized by family membership. Some experts suggest releasing these individuals, as they would certainly be recognized by the members of their family and accepted back into the fold.

One of the most extensively studied groups of cetaceans in the world is that of the killer whales who frequent the area around the island of Vancouver. In Canadian waters and in the waters immediately adjacent to the state of Washington, there are probably a total of 250 animals. Each of these animals has been given a code and a name; in fact, since individuals can be identified by the shape of the white spots, especially those right behind the dorsal fin, researchers are also able to follow their movements. As the photographs illustrate, killer whales execute leaps and acrobatics, and this is the aspect of their behavior that most closely links them to their dolphin "cousins."

whales are often capable of swimming up rivers for hundreds of miles, unhindered by the differences in salinity of fresh water. In 1931, a young female killer whale swam 110 nautical miles up the Columbia River in Oregon, as far inland as the city of Portland; in Scotland, another killer whale was observed hunting ducks in the Firth of Forth, and all through the last century, before industrial pollution and motorized shipping began on a massive scale, killer whales were often seen swimming in the Thames, the Loire, the Seine, the Elbe, and the Rhine—in short, in the heart of Europe. And once they were spotted, they were regularly harpooned and slaughtered. Killer whales have historically avoided being hunted because—like almost all of the toothed whales except for the sperm whale—they have little or nothing to offer by way of oil, baleen, meat, and other raw materials. Certainly, they have not been left alone out of fear, because a killer whale could cause little concern to a steel-hulled ship armed with a harpoon-launching cannon such as those used regularly in hunting baleen whales.

Over the past decade, however, since strict regulations have been applied to whaling, the killer whale, too, has been added to humanity's hit list. Once the other large whales had been hunted down and their populations decimated, the chief whaling nations—in particular, Russia, Norway, Iceland, and Japan—began to massacre killer whales. A killer whale yields no more than three quarters of a ton of oil; this is very little compared to the bounty of a right whale or blue whale. It appears, however, that the Russians know how to obtain a very fine oil from the jaw of these cetaceans, and this oil is incomparable for lubricating precision machinery. The skin of killer whales can be used to make collagen fiber for the soles of shoes. The meat (heretofore prized as food only by the Makah Indians of Canada and the natives of the Commander Islands in the Bering Sea) is usually ground up and used as animal feed.

In the meantime, however, humanity has made another "useful" discovery—killer whales can be captured alive without enormous difficulty and they are well suited to life in captivity. After watching killer whales in captivity, humans have learned that they are very sociable and capable of learning and performing an endless variety of aquatic games and tricks. This opportunity to learn more about the animals' behavior has been a boon to science. Most likely, many years will have to pass before anyone decides to give this animal a less ominous scientific name. At least we're headed in the right direction.

As far as food is concerned, killer whales will not refuse anything edible that is found in the sea. In some regions, they tend to concentrate on fish such as salmon, while in other areas they attack sea birds such as penguins, and even other cetaceans—they have been known even to attack rorqual whales. In any case, and certainly when the prey is large, close cooperation among the members of the group is required. The dietary habits of killer whales and their marked sociability are in some way connected, because group hunting requires coordination and trust between individuals. Each pod, or family group, is generally made up of a female and her descendants, and offspring spend their entire lives in the pod to which their mother belonged. In the photograph on the right, a male killer whale is shown catching a ray near the island of Santa Cruz in the Galapagos.

Playa de la Punta Norte, Valdés Peninsula, Argentina. A rare glimpse of a killer whale capturing prey on land. In this sequence, a young male swims onto a beach populated by sea lions. The adults manage to flee while the large predator emerges almost entirely from the water, seizes one of the young, and carries it off. Still more discon-certing is the fact that, once it is in the open waters, the killer whale does not immediately kill the unfortunate pup, but seems to play with it, tossing it into the air with blows of its tail. In reality, this is not gratuitous cruelty—the techniques of hunting must be learned, and perhaps playing with live prey helps the young killer whale to practice.

BELUGAS

The white cetaceans known as belugas live in the cold waters of the Arctic. They belong (along with narwhals) to a family all their own, that of the Monodontidae. Unlike most other cetaceans, belugas are endowed with a certain mobility of the neck which allows them to turn their heads. They are also known as the "canaries of the sea," because they possess a vast repertoire of sounds with which they communicate; in some cases these whistles and clicks, accompanied by violent gnashing of the jaws, can even be heard above the surface of the water.

PAGES 88-89
The head of the beluga is surmounted by a large "melon," a protuberance that is found in other toothed whales and which is probably useful in biosonar, an echolocation system.

PAGES 90-91
In the summer, belugas tend to congregate in certain bays near the estuaries of northern rivers.

The name *beluga* comes from the Russian word for "white"—*bielo*. The beluga is born dark gray in color, lightens to a mottled yellow during the early years of its life, and becomes completely white between its fourth and ninth year. The beluga and the narwhal are the only two species in the family of Monodontidae. In the beluga (*Delphinapterus leucas*), the cervical vertebrae are not joined, and as a result, these cetaceans enjoy a certain mobility of the neck and can rotate their heads independently of their body. In schools of between five and ten individuals, they are scattered along the coasts of the Arctic and adjoining waters; they tend to prefer deep fjords, bays, and the mouths of rivers toward the open sea. At times, single specimens push south as far as the North Sea and the Baltic Sea. When one was found in the Black Sea in the summer of 1992, it was guessed that the white whale must have escaped from some dolphin show, because in order to make its way to the Black Sea, the white whale would have had to swim along the Atlantic Coast of France, Spain, and Portugal and swim across the entire Mediterranean. There was a full-fledged outpouring of international solidarity, and environmentalists and animal protectionists captured the beluga and returned it to its chilly natural environment.

In 1966, something similar happened when, on 15 May, in the Rhine River near Nijmegen, Holland, a beluga was spotted for the first time ever. The snowy cetacean reappeared three days later in Duisburg, Germany. The director of the city zoo there, Doctor Wolfgang Gewalt, worked for two weeks to capture the whale, concerned that the animal's long journey through muddy river waters must have weakened it and caused it to fall sick. But to no avail—the beluga, which at first had been easy to approach and trusting, became suspicious and elusive. It continued to swim up the Rhine and, on 12 and 13 June, was spotted in Bonn, and on 14 June at Bad Honnef. Then it began to swim very quickly downstream and, on 16 June, exactly a month after the beginning of its adventure, it swam past Rotterdam and out into the Atlantic Ocean at the Hook of Holland.

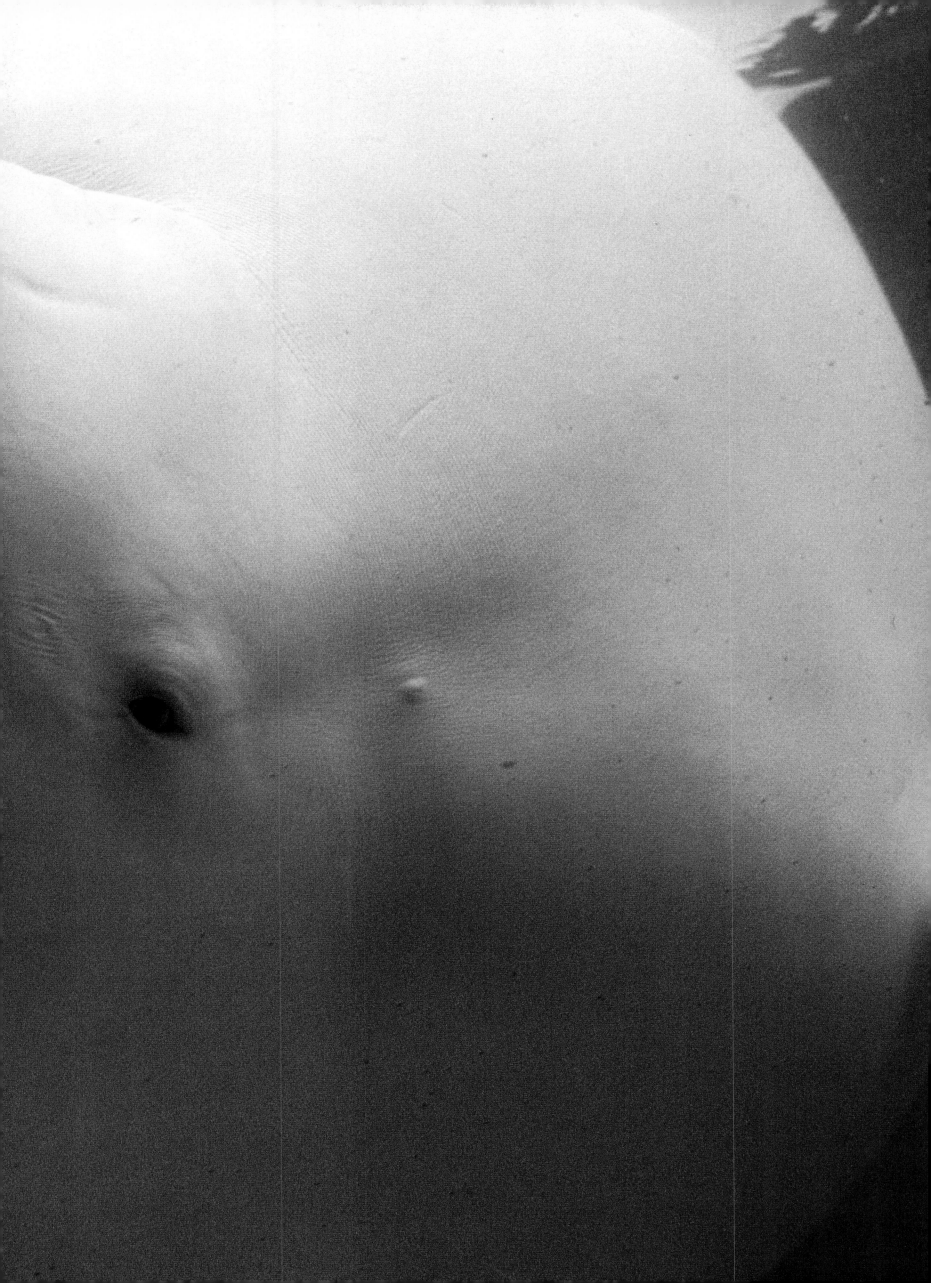

NARWHALS

The young of the narwhal are practically identical to the young of the beluga; their adult body structure and length (16 feet at the most) are quite similar. All that varies is the color of the skin, which is grayish and spotted in the narwhal, and the teeth. The narwhal takes its scientific name (*Monodon monoceros*) from its most evident physical feature: a single, spiraled tusk which may have inspired the legend of the unicorn. Found only in the males, the tusk is believed to be a secondary sexual characteristic; its length apparently serves to establish a hierarchy among males. It does not serve to frighten off the killer whale, the only animal that includes the narwhal in its diet.

The only humans who eat narwhals are Eskimos, but they eat only the skin, which is rich in nutrition. "Civilized" humans have long sought the narwhal for the blubber, from which they obtain a very fine oil, well suited to lubricating precision instruments, and of course for the ivory found in its very unusual tusk. The tusk, which can reach nine feet in length, develops from one of the narwhal's two teeth, usually the left; in some cases, however, the right tusk also grows in a disproportionate manner, in which case this harmless animal acquires a truly frightening appearance. In medieval times, the ivory of the huge tusk of the narwhal was often foisted off as the magical horn of the mythical unicorn, and it was worth far more than its weight in gold.

When humanity was finally convinced that the unicorn did not exist, the narwhal was still hunted down, but in a far more haphazard fashion. It fell victim to the hunters of right whales off Greenland and in the Arctic. Then, when this type of whaling came to an end, the narwhal was finally left in peace. Only the Eskimos continue to hunt narwhals; they sell the tusks to tourists and find numerous uses for the tendons and skin. Today, unfortunately, the Inuit, with the assistance of modern technology, are threatening the existence of narwhals, more so than they did when, with rudimentary weapons, they hunted only a few for food.

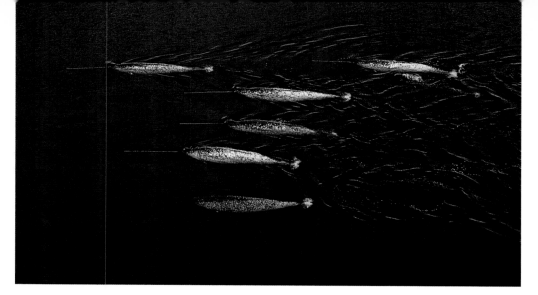

Only male narwhals have the distinctive spiral tusk, in reality an overgrown tooth. The fact that the tip is always smooth and polished, without any encrusted algae, leads us to think that the unusual structure is used regularly, probably in combat between males.

PILOT WHALES

Like the other members of its genus, the pilot whale (*Globicephala melas*—one of the largest members of the dolphin family) lives in schools of hundreds of individuals, often following a single leader. The whale-hunting inhabitants of the Faer Øer islands know their habits well; when they spot a school, they approach cautiously and wound one or two of the whales, then drag them (if they've harpooned them) or push them (if they've shot them with rifles) onto the shore, where the other pilot whales then beach themselves and lie at the hunters' mercy. What the islanders obtain from the pilot whales is their precious oil; they freeze the meat and sell it to pet food manufacturers; they grind the bones for chicken feed.

Tragically, pilot whales often beach themselves and thus become condemned to certain death from overheating, being slowly crushed by their own weight, or drowning when the tide covers their blowholes. That whales beach themselves is a curiosity of nature—one which has been studied by zoologists for years. What happens to the lead whale? What happens to the others, that they blindly follow it toward dry land and throw themselves onto the fatal shore, even when we try to drag them back into the water and push them out to sea?

One of these mysterious collective "suicides" occurred in Jacksonville, Florida, in 1977. Hundreds of whales beached themselves near the naval base of Mayport. All of the efforts of rescuers who rushed to help them get back to sea proved useless. Even when the pilot whales were taken to open water, they would swim doggedly back to shore until they lay dying on the hot sand. Some speculated that their behavior was a result of pollution or of nuclear testing. But those who sought the true explanation were the marine biologists and zoologists who rushed to the scene to examine the bodies.

They performed autopsies and took tissue samples. Specialists from the Smithsonian were sent in, but by the time they arrived, the bodies were so badly decomposed that they could not extract any reliable scientific information. The unhappy conclusion of the event caused considerable dispute and debate, and the cause of the tragedy—natural or unnatural—remains unknown.

A great many mass beachings of pilot whales have occurred in recent years. Many people have worked in vain to return these creatures to the sea to keep them from killing themselves. Others have taken advantage of the "gift of nature" and actually accelerated the death of the animals by clubbing them to death and cutting them into pieces on the beach. Still, we know no more than we did the first time a beaching was recorded; when they beach themselves, these creatures are exhibiting a baffling behavior.

We might wonder whether these whales are without intelligence—exceptions in the family Delphinidae (all other members are considered bright). But that is not the case: pilot whales raised in captivity have demonstrated considerable learning ability, proving to be the equals of their cousins in performing the tasks assigned to them by humans. Pilot whales can even be trained to respond to a series of modulated whistles; it is amusing to watch them perform leaps and pirouettes in the marine parks. They have also been trained by the military—to do tasks previously performed only by dolphins or other small, toothed whales. They've helped rescue sailors trapped in crippled submarines, detected and recovered mines and other unexploded ordnance, and echolocated enemy ordnance.

Pilot whales, which are broken down into two quite similar species, are from 13 to 20 feet long. Dark in color, with a white pattern on the belly, they are known to assemble in groups of hundreds at a time, although it is more common to find them in groups of a few dozen. The cohesion of the group is particularly strong among pilot whales, and humans have often taken advantage of this tendency in hunting them. Even today, in the Faer Øer Islands, located in the Atlantic midway between Norway and Iceland, these animals are driven toward the shore and massacred. The pilot whale is one of the species that is most frequently beached en masse; the phenomenon still constitutes a mystery, but perhaps it occurs when the group follows one of the animals in difficulty, even though as a result they all become beached and die.

PAGES 98-99
A closeup of a pilot whale in the waters off the Hawaiian Islands. These cetaceans often display curiosity toward humans.

This photograph shows the entrance of the grotto, which is about 50 feet under water. In order to reach the skeletons of the pilot whales, it is necessary to swim another 300 feet or so.

Near the island of Matagi in the Fiji Islands, a remarkable underwater cemetery has been discovered; an entire school of pilot whales seems to have come to die in an underwater grotto 150 feet below the surface. In this very limited space, the bones of a number of different pilot whales have been found. On the left, one can see a large skull, illuminated by the diver; some two-and-a-half feet across, it probably belonged to the lead whale. In the image on the right, we can see the skulls of a young pilot whale and of an adult, perhaps its mother. These two skeletons were found at a depth of nearly 70 feet in the last room of the grotto, more than 600 feet from the heart of the reef. Only hypotheses can be ventured concerning the causes of this singular collective demise of pilot whales. These whales are known for elevated levels of social behavior and also for the tendency to die in groups on beaches. Perhaps they entered the grotto while fleeing some predator; perhaps the young whale became lost and the group followed it. In any case, the whales must have become trapped in a space too narrow to turn around in and drowned.

A false killer whale, a cetacean in the family Delphinidae, is shown devouring a dolphin fish in the waters off the Hawaiian Islands. This species feeds chiefly on cephalopods and large fish and at times steals prey from fishermen's nets. It is said that false killer whales also attack other small cetaceans. Like pilot whales, which they resemble, they are extremely gregarious, forming groups ranging in size from a dozen to several hundred individuals. This species also falls victim to mass beachings.

DOLPHINS

Among the most representative and elegant of all Delphinidae are the striped dolphins, which are generally found in all temperate, subtropical, and tropical seas; in the Mediterranean, they are the most common cetaceans. They can be recognized by, among other things, the characteristic white "brush- *strokes" that start from their eyes and run down their sides. In the oceans especially, striped dolphins are found in groups of hundreds and at times even thousands of individuals. Striped dolphins often accompany fast ships, from speedboats to passenger liners, bowriding and leaping alongside acrobatically.*

I remember the terrified confusion of mothers and fishermen one afternoon when a black fin cut through the water just off the little port of Mergellina near Naples. The mothers were sure that this was a shark, but it was only a dolphin that had come to play near the shore, unaware of the presence of humans and of the terrible danger that they represented. Fishermen in the Mediterranean and in other seas around the world are not fond of dolphins. They consider dolphins to be "bad fish" because they compete in the hunt for "good fish." And, especially in the Mediterranean, fishermen hunt down dolphins in order to obtain *musciame*, a sort of dolphin-meat jerky, which they obtain by slicing the meat very fine and then hanging it out from the yardarms of their boats, letting the wind and sun cook it slowly. Since dolphins are a protected species and killing them is against the law almost everywhere in the world, the captains of the fishing boats invariably claim—if they are caught red-handed with a load of dolphin meat—that the big, intelligent mammals simply got tangled in their nets and drowned.

This is, in fact, what often happens. One of the biggest and most repeated massacres of dolphins occurs in the eastern Pacific Ocean during the tuna fishing season. The instrument of death is the drift net. Fishing boats guided by helicopters surround the schools of tuna in the open ocean with nets that are miles long. Swimming above the schools of tuna, for reasons that have not yet been fully understood, are dolphins. And the dolphins are slaughtered along with the tuna, or else they are caught in the mesh of the nets and drown. This type of massacre dates back to ancient times. Aristotle complained about the way in which *hoi barbaroi*—anyone who did not speak Greek—would capture dolphins by pounding on the water with oars and tossing great stones into the sea. This strange way of hunting dolphins is used all over the world; it seems to work because the noise interferes with the system of echolocation used by dolphins to find their way around.

For the peoples of Oceania, the dolphin is sacred to the gods, and it would be a serious sacrilege to kill one. Unless, of course, the dolphin were to offer itself up voluntarily. In that case, of course, the dolphin hunt—for that is what it is, under the guise of a sacred ritual—would simply become a propitiatory rite in honor of a sacred and benign victim that voluntarily offers to sacrifice itself. As soon as the dolphins appear off the coast, men and women hop into their outrigger canoes and paddle out toward

them, while others wait on shore. All the people standing on shore and paddling canoes chant out a song of welcome, to the bounding beat of paddles and rocks on and beneath the surface of the water. The ultrasensitive hearing of the dolphins is rendered inoperative by these vibrations pouring in from all directions and from the entire span of the semicircle defined by the islanders in canoes. The dolphins surface in search of some respite, and this behavior is interpreted as an offering, a self-sacrifice, which the islanders hasten to accept.

Today, the various species of dolphins are protected by many international agreements, but the authorities of the great nations of the Atlantic and Pacific—especially the United States and Australia—are unable to exert absolute control over the fishing fleets that continue to slaughter thousands of dolphins each year in order to bring in harvests of tuna and other fish. Nor can the authorities simply bombard and sink the fishing boats from Japan and other nations that continue to hunt these protected species.

And yet, deep in the roots of civilization, there is an ancient veneration and respect for dolphins. To the ancient Greeks, the dolphin was a living symbol of life in the sea and of the link between water and life in general. For the Eskimos, too, even though they hunt whales of all sizes, the whale is neither enemy nor monster, but rather a benevolent creature that may test their mettle as hunters but in the end yields its bounty and allows them the gift of survival.

Perhaps the best known of all dolphins is the bottle-nosed dolphin, which is the dolphin most often seen in aquariums and dolphin shows. The reason that this species adapts better to captivity than all the others is that in the wild, bottle-nosed dolphins tend to frequent coastal waters, where the water is shallow and the environmental conditions (such as temperature and salinity of the water) are variable, much as is the case in a pool. Today, however, not everyone agrees that wild creatures should be kept in captivity, all the more because it is now possible to document the life of animals in their natural habitat. Bottle-nosed dolphins have been known to fish in collaboration with humans; in Mauritania, the local fishermen are regularly assisted by bottle-nosed dolphins who drive fish into the nets.

In the waters of the Bahamas, a group of spotted dolphins has become quite accustomed over the years to the presence of snorkelers and scuba divers who periodically come to visit them, stopping for a while to play. The size and number of spots on the bodies of the various individual animals are quite variable and allow divers to distinguish one from the other fairly easily.

PAGES 110-111
This is Jo-Jo, a bottle-nosed dolphin who swims in the waters of the island of Providenciales in the Turks and Caicos Islands; he has "made friends" with human beings, and regularly allows them to approach him.

CETACEAN LIFE *Maddalena Jahoda*

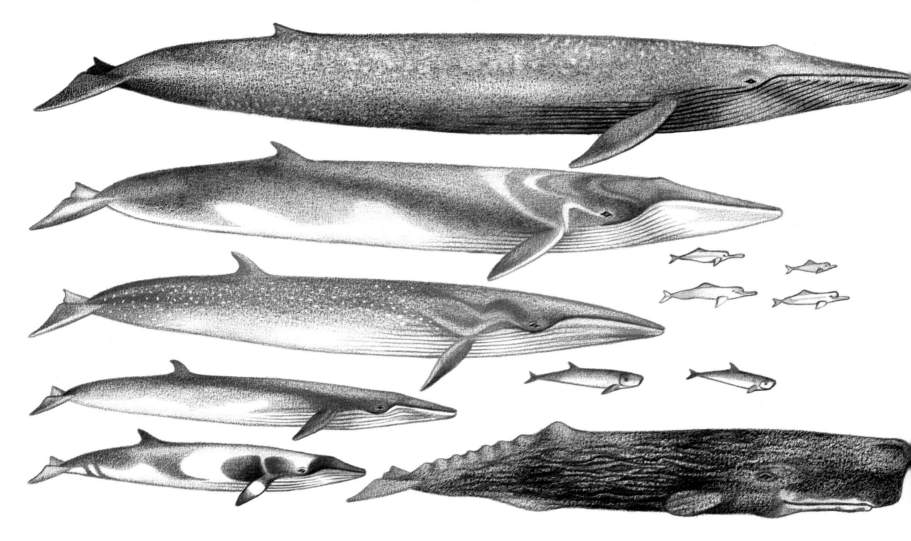

From Aristotle onward, there has been an endless series of misconceptions concerning the classification of cetaceans. The reason is that these animals have some of the finest "camouflage" in the world—they are mammals disguised as fish. Today we know that despite the presence of flippers, the fishlike body, and a number of features involved in adaptation to their underwater environment, whales are warm-blooded creatures, whales breathe air, and female whales give birth to live young and suckle them. Yet a number of mysteries surrounding cetaceans remain. This group of animals remains one of the most difficult to study and at the same time one of the most fascinating and perplexing. To date, 78 species of cetaceans have been identified, and they are very different from one another, although they share specific features. The most evident of these features is the streamlined, fishlike shape of their bodies, which enables them to swim with minimal resistance. The ancestors of cetaceans lived on land before moving into the sea.

The constraints of the environment in which they now live, in conjunction with the basic characteristics of a mammal, combine to offer a fairly concise picture of just how a cetacean "works." One of their basic requirements is to return to the surface on a regular basis in order to replenish their supply of air. Inhaling and exhaling is accomplished through a blowhole, a type of nostril located atop the head in the very spot that first emerges from the water. This blowhole is, to all intents and purposes, a "nose" which is also endowed with a closure that seals the opening as soon as the cetacean dives under water. This is not the only organ that has a human counterpart but which has been modified out of necessity. The pectoral fins, or flippers, for example, constitute an adaptation of the front legs of cetaceans' terrestrial ancestors; the skeleton of the flipper greatly resembles that of our hands. The rear limbs, on the other hand, have been lost. The organ that provides propulsion is the horizontal tail fin, or fluke. It moves up and down and propels the

whale through the water. The unique orientation of the tail makes it possible to distinguish a cetacean from a fish at first glance; cetaceans have horizontal tails and fish have vertical tails.

Other modifications have occurred which ensure total hydrodynamic efficiency, such as the absence of hair on the body and the absence of other protruding appendages such as ears. Instead of hair, which serves to preserve heat in the bodies of other mammals, there is a thick mantle of blubber which allows cetaceans to keep their body temperatures elevated and quite constant, no matter how cold the water in which they are swimming. This system is so effective that there are cetaceans in every sea in the world, including both polar oceans.

Whales and dolphins can perform remarkable feats during extended stays under water. A sperm whale, for instance, can stay under water without breathing for as long as two hours and at remarkable depths; their oxygen is then replenished when they surface. Various forms of physiological adaptation make this pos-

sible, including the capacity to store oxygen in the muscles and to reroute the oxygenated blood to the organs that have the greatest need, such as the heart and the brain.

Even greater difficulties arise for a mammal that lives underwater during reproduction; in fact, seals and sea lions, which are also sea mammals, come to land for reproduction—both for mating and for the birth of their young. Cetaceans are the only group of sea mammals that carry out the entire biological cycle of reproduction in the water. As soon as the newborn cetacean emerges from its mother's body, it must swim to the surface and take a breath of air within minutes. If the newborn does not immediately do so, then its mother and the other cetaceans in the school will help it by pushing it up toward the surface. This instinctive action, as we shall see, appears elsewhere in the "psychology" of the cetaceans, which are often observed keeping afloat a fellow cetacean in trouble (and in some cases, even a human being).

Even though whales and dolphins are

similar in terms of their physiology, there are a great many categories of cetaceans. There are the toothed whales, which have conical teeth in one or both jaws and feed on fish and squid, and baleen whales, which have plates of whalebone on the side of the upper jaw for filtering plankton from the water. The second group includes right whales, gray whales, and rorquals, which together constitute the majority of large cetaceans. Their prime identifying feature is the presence of whalebones, or baleen—long slabs of a material similar to human fingernails—that hang from the palate and serve to filter plankton from seawater. In the suborder of baleen whales, there are five species of rorqual whales: the humpback whale, the gray whale, the "right" whales (the southern and northern right whales), the bowhead whale, and the pygmy right whale. The toothed whales include six families, among which are dolphins, beluga whales and narwhals, the sperm whale and two smaller relatives, beaked whales, saltwater porpoises, and their freshwater counterparts.

The classification of cetaceans, like that of a great many other animals, is undergoing constant change and modification. From time to time, new species are discovered, while other species are reassigned to a different group. For instance, it may surprise the reader to learn that the pilot whale is classified as a dolphin, while porpoises, to all appearances similar to dolphins, are in a group all their own. These remarkable animals never cease to amaze those who study them. A great many surprising new discoveries will probably emerge in the lifetimes of those now devoted to observing and understanding cetaceans.

In the chapters that follow, we have chosen, from the many species, a few of the ones which best serve to illustrate the most fascinating aspects of the biology of cetaceans.

EVOLUTION

The origin of the cetaceans remains a bit of a mystery, a story with a great many unclear twists, the plot of which can only be reconstructed through a few clues, primarily fossil fragments. The ancestors of cetaceans were small, carnivorous, land-based quadrupeds, which belonged to the family Mesonichidae, a family that was to generate yet another group of modern mammals, the ungulates (hoofed mammals). This means that deer, oxen, and horses are all cousins to cetaceans, and this improbable relation is confirmed by the composition of their blood and by other biochemical similarities. Considering, however, that horses and whales appear to have little in common, a considerable

transformation must have taken place in the course of the evolution of the cetaceans.

In the mosaic that has been painstakingly reconstructed of the origin of the cetaceans, a crucial piece of the puzzle was missing. The fossils of the land-based ancestors, the Mesonichidae, were available, as well as those of the primitive whales, or Archaeoceti, which were already well adapted to the marine environment, but no fossils survived to show the nature of the transition from land to sea. The missing link was found in 1981 in Pakistan. It was *Pakicetus inachus*, the most ancient cetacean ever found. The study of this fossil casts new light onto the research being done by paleontologists to recon-

struct the history of the order, a history that spans geological eras, in which each transition is measured in millions of years. *Pakicetus* lived more than 50 million years ago, and during that time several crucial changes occurred. In the shallow lagoons and the slow waters of the tropical regions, the ancestors of the cetaceans splashed about in coastal waters. They were already partially adapted to living in water, but they maintained the ears and dentition of land animals. Their bodies, however, were already elongated, their rear limbs were diminishing, and their snouts had already begun to protrude. These animals at first probably fed on the mollusks and crustaceans they found in the mud and

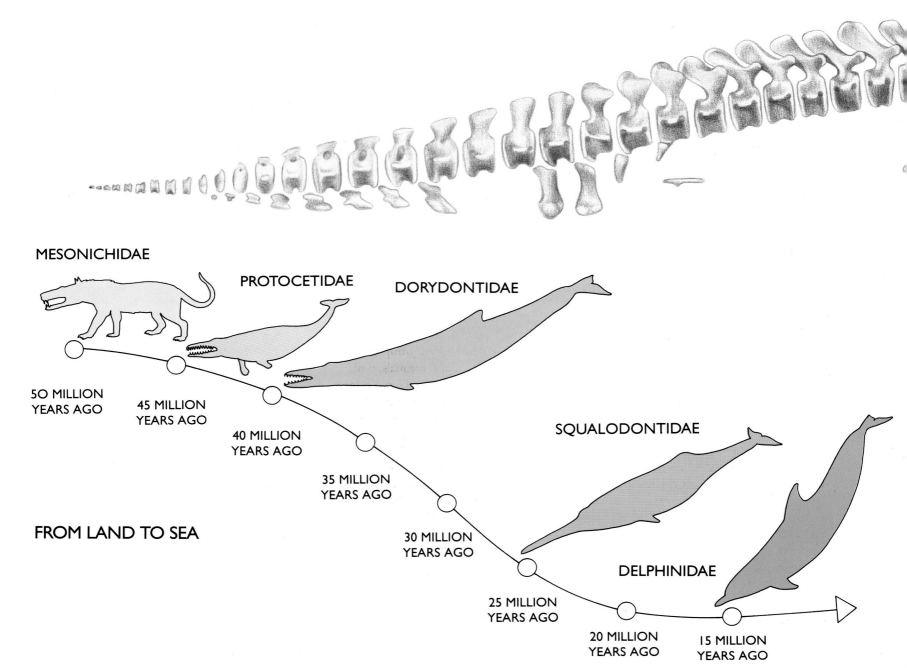

MESONICHIDAE

PROTOCETIDAE

DORYDONTIDAE

SQUALODONTIDAE

DELPHINIDAE

FROM LAND TO SEA

50 MILLION YEARS AGO

45 MILLION YEARS AGO

40 MILLION YEARS AGO

35 MILLION YEARS AGO

30 MILLION YEARS AGO

25 MILLION YEARS AGO

20 MILLION YEARS AGO

15 MILLION YEARS AGO

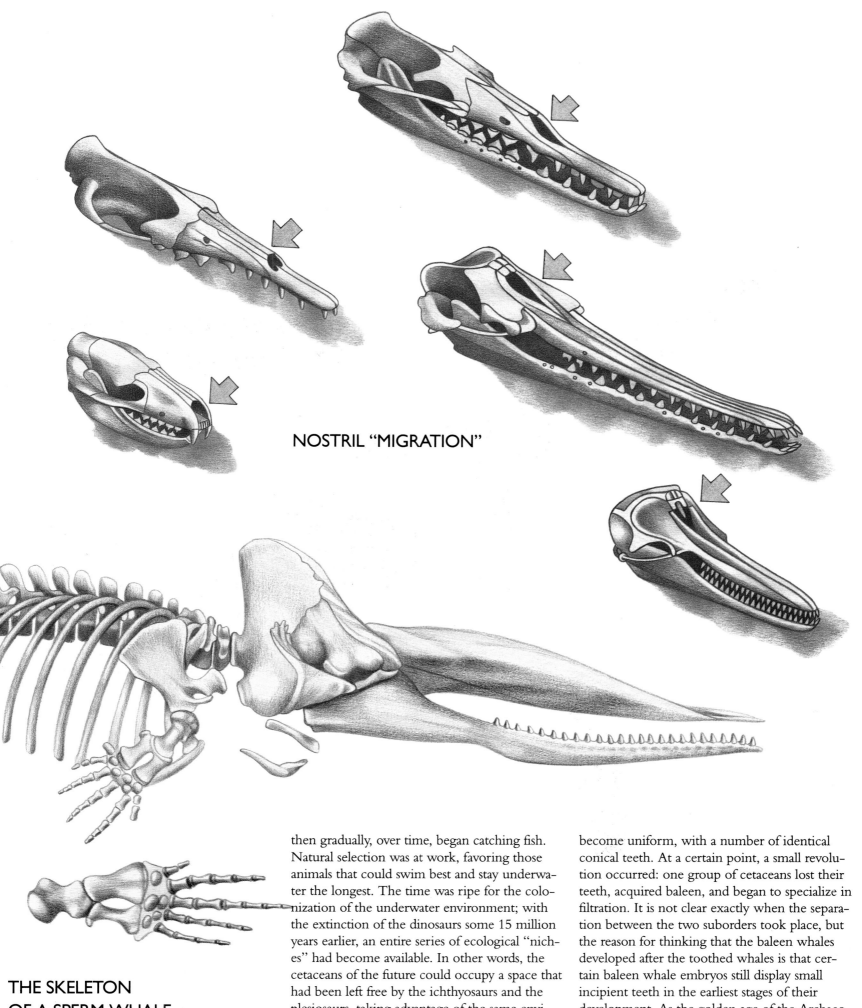

NOSTRIL "MIGRATION"

THE SKELETON
OF A SPERM WHALE

then gradually, over time, began catching fish. Natural selection was at work, favoring those animals that could swim best and stay underwater the longest. The time was ripe for the colonization of the underwater environment; with the extinction of the dinosaurs some 15 million years earlier, an entire series of ecological "niches" had become available. In other words, the cetaceans of the future could occupy a space that had been left free by the ichthyosaurs and the plesiosaurs, taking advantage of the same environmental resources.

The Archaeoceti began to differentiate into a number of different species, each with a set of individual adaptations. In all of them, however, the skull elongated even further forward, the nostrils migrated from the tip of the snout back to the top of the head, and a broad, flat tail developed. The rear limbs disappeared and the forelimbs changed definitively into flippers. Lastly, the dentition changed, tending to

become uniform, with a number of identical conical teeth. At a certain point, a small revolution occurred: one group of cetaceans lost their teeth, acquired baleen, and began to specialize in filtration. It is not clear exactly when the separation between the two suborders took place, but the reason for thinking that the baleen whales developed after the toothed whales is that certain baleen whale embryos still display small incipient teeth in the earliest stages of their development. As the golden age of the Archaeoceti ended and the group was dying out some 30 or 40 million years ago, a great many other species of modern cetaceans were developing, destined to survive into the future.

HUMPBACK WHALE
Megaptera novaeangliae

AVERAGE SIZE

Newborns:	14–16 feet
Adults:	(females) 50 feet
	(males) 45 feet
	Weight: 33–50 tons

Among the whales most often described and photographed, humpbacks can be recognized by their knobby snouts and their very long pectoral flippers not unlike a pair of wings. These flippers measure nearly a third of the length of the humpback's body (up to 50 feet in an adult), are usually white on the lower surface and at times on the upper surface as well; the edges of the flippers are also covered with knobs (which offer easy access to a great many skin parasites). On the back of the humpback stands a small dorsal fin which varies widely in shape. Just in front of the fin is a small hump, hence the whale's name. The humpback is put in the same family as the rorqual whales, though the physical resemblance is not clearly evident. The humpback is far less streamlined, but its overall shape, its ventral grooves, and the narrow silhouette of the head in some way link it to the genus Balaenoptera. Humpbacks tend to move in small groups of

three or four and do not seem to have particularly strong social ties. The possibility should not, however, be ruled out that individuals keep in acoustical contact even at considerable distances. This species, in fact, makes ample use of vocal communication, to the point that during the mating season, the males perform lengthy "songs," some of the most complex in the animal kingdom. The significance of these songs has yet to be puzzled out, but in all likelihood, they have to do with courtship and sexual competition. The majority of studies have dealt with the humpbacks of the northern Pacific Ocean, a great many of whom spend the winter in the waters off Hawaii and the summer around Alaska and Siberia. In the Atlantic Ocean, too, they have been studied carefully; the Atlantic humpbacks tend to move between the Caribbean and the eastern coast of the United States and Canada. They always follow extremely precise routes

in their migrations, and the same is true of the humpbacks of the southern hemisphere, whose summer grounds are situated in the Antarctic seas and whose winters grounds are the coasts of Africa and Australia. Humpbacks live in practically all of the seas and oceans of the planet and at all latitudes, from tropical waters to polar waters, though today the population has been drastically decimated by the whaling to which the humpbacks have been subjected for many decades. Although they are now a protected species, they do not seem to be recovering substantially; it is calculated that of the 15,000 humpbacks that were believed to live in the Pacific before the advent of industrialized whaling, today no more than 1,000 survive. And out of the 150,000 humpbacks that once swam the planet, there are now estimated to be no more than 25,000 alive today.

WHY DO THEY LEAP?

At Silver Bank, just north of the Caribbean island of Hispaniola, a humpback whale once attracted the attention of researchers in the area. In just 75 minutes, it made no fewer than 130 leaps out of the water. This leaping is not uncommon; a number of cetacean species have the habit of soaring out of the water, twisting in the air, and then producing spectacular belly-flops. When a whale belly-flops, it drops the weight of 477 humans with an average weight of 155 pounds onto the water's surface.

Why do whales leap? This is a question that has been widely debated, and a great number of possible explanations have been offered. Dolphins, too, leap when they travel on the surface; in their case it would seem to be a method for lessening water resistance. For large cetaceans, this explanation cannot be applied; humpbacks, for instance, do not move forward when they leap, but tend to fall back to the water in the same spot from which they emerged. Their leaping seems to have little to do with travel and much more to do with social interaction—in particular, with sexual reproduction. Generally, baleen whales tend to gather for reproduction in the winter, living on the fat they have accumulated over the summer. The distinction between breeding season and feeding season is sharper in certain "fatter" species. Other cetaceans, such as the rorqual whales, have a more flexible annual schedule, and they may feed more constantly (and they are therefore more streamlined, accumulating less fat), are less socially active and do less leaping. This is one theory that has been advanced, but certainly not the only one. For instance, it would also seem that humpbacks do more leaping when boats are present. Therefore, it is believed that the leaping is a display of aggression unleashed by the presence of threatening objects or a response to the noise of the engines. Not everyone agrees with this interpretation; the leaps could also be interpreted as a form of communication. In fact, the sound of a humpback leaping and then slapping down onto the water could have a precise meaning to the other humpbacks down below.

Humpbacks and southern right whales tend to do their leaping in groups; when one leaps, the others are likely to imitate it, so that there might be a vast array of leaping whales for miles and miles. It also seems, at least within certain limits, that humpbacks do more leaping when the wind is blowing. One possible explanation for this is that the leaping could serve as communication, especially when the sounds of the wind prevent the whales from hearing one another. One other possible explanation is that this is nothing more than playfulness. This hypothesis is corroborated by the observation that young humpbacks are already leaping out of the water at the age of just a few weeks. But why should the adults waste energy on this? It has been calculated that a whale leaping out of the water consumes about 250 kilocalories, about a hundredth of their energy supply for an entire day. A series of leaps requires a considerable expenditure of energy. One possibility is that, in the mating season, males leap in order to demonstrate to the females that they are the most vigorous. If we decide to look in a radically different direction, however, we can imagine that the impact of a giant belly-flop onto the water might give the animal temporary relief from the parasites on its skin. Or they might simply leap to take a look around; the frequent twisting would allow them to sweep the horizon with their eyes. That would explain why they leap more frequently in the presence of something that piques their curiosity, such as boats. Finally, whales may leap as a way of emphasizing a message—a 35-ton animal leaping out of the water is certainly eloquent, whatever it may be trying to say.

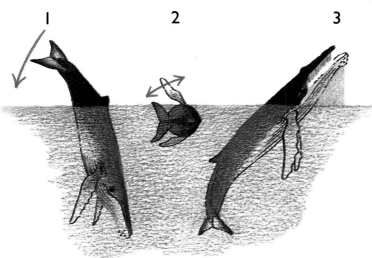

The "aerial" behavior of the humpback, the most acrobatic of all the baleen whales, is quite distinctive. They have several typical behaviors—a blow from the fluke (1) or pectoral flipper (2) and the emergence of the upper body from the surface of the water (3).

As for full-fledged leaping, there are several types. The humpback can emerge at all different angles up to 70 degrees from the surface of the water; in the twisting leap (4), it falls on its back, while in the common leap, it falls to the water with a belly-flop (5). The entire sequence of the twisting leap appears at bottom (6).

1

2

3

4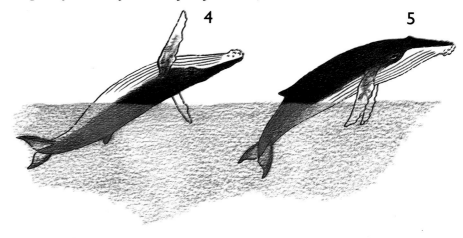

5

6

SPECIES	RATIO OF MASS TO LENGTH CUBED	FREQUENCY OF LEAPS
Humpback Whale *Megaptera novaengliae*	10:6	Very Frequent
Southern Right Whale *Eubalaena australis*	16:2	Frequent
Gray Whale *Eschrichtius robustus*	14:3	Frequent
Sperm Whale *Physeter catodon*	10:7/19:1	Frequent
Bowhead Whale *Balaena mysticetus*	26:7	Infrequent
Bryde's Whale *Balaenoptera edeni*	6:1	Infrequent
Minke Whale *Balaenoptera acutorostrata*	12:3	Very Infrequent
Fin Whale *Balaenoptera physalus*	4:0	Extremely Infrequent
Blue Whale *Balaenoptera musculus*	6:3	Almost Never
Sei Whale *Balaenoptera borealis*	3:6	Almost Never

A study conducted by the cetologist Hal Whitehead would seem to indicate that, contrary to what one might expect, less streamlined whales leap more often. As this chart shows, the stout humpbacks and right whales leap more frequently than their streamlined cousins, the rorquals.

FISHING WITH BUBBLES

The filtering cetaceans, which is to say, the baleen whales, have been described as great grazers of the sea inasmuch as they simply open their mouths and gather anything that swims into them. In reality, this is not a precise description, at least if we are to judge from one of the techniques adopted by the humpbacks who, in a certain sense, actively "fish." Indeed, these whales build themselves a "net" made out of air bubbles that they release from their blowholes, lasting just the time needed to capture small fish and plankton. The phenomenon was first described by whalers at the turn of the century who had seen, in the waters off Greenland, mysterious bubbles on the surface, arranged in a perfect circle. Since mariners are well known for tall tales, however, no one gave much credence to their accounts.

In 1979, however, a small scientific expedition went to Glacier Bay in Alaska to study the summer feeding grounds of the humpbacks. These scientists observed the phenomenon of the bubble rings, and the researchers formulated

for the first time an interpretation that these must have been humpbacks feeding. The technique the humpbacks employed was to dive deep and then swim up in a spiral, all the while releasing a steady stream of air from their blowholes. The result was a sort of cone of air, narrow at the bottom and gradually wider toward the surface, generally measuring 13 to 16 feet across. In some cases, the "net" was as broad as 100 feet, which may indicate cooperation among several whales. The bubbles, which rise in a steady stream, form a sort of cage, and fish and plankton, frightened by the noise and confusion, tend to huddle in the center. The most impressive sight, however, comes a few moments later, just instants after the bubbles first appear. Amid the rumble and hiss of the escaping air, the enormous gaping jaws of the humpback suddenly explode out of the water, and its ventral grooves expand as the whale gulps down an enormous mouthful of water and plankton and small fish.

A further confirmation that the net of bubbles is actually used by the humpback to procure food has been obtained by sampling the organisms present in the water inside and outside of the circle. On the inside, the concentration of plankton was indeed much higher. One question remains unsolved, however: do the humpbacks induce their tiny prey to cluster together, or do they simply choose an area where the krill are already densely concentrated, then cast a net around them to keep them from scattering? The answer has not been found, but a further indication of the humpback's enterprising nature is that they seem to be capable of emitting bubbles of various sizes depending on the size of their prey. And that's not all—while they are creating their net of bubbles, they also emit rhythmic sounds. Through a hydrophone —an electrical instrument for detecting and monitoring sound under water—it is possible to listen to the sound, which is not a deafening roar, as one might expect from a "leviathan," but rather sounds like the hiss of an old steam kettle.

GRAY WHALE

Eschrichtius robustus

AVERAGE SIZE

Newborns:	15 feet
Adults:	45 feet
Weight:	30-37 tons

THE GREAT MIGRATION

The pointed and slightly downward-curving snout gives this species a distinctive silhouette. Likewise, the gray color of the body, with small white and yellowish spots, makes it easy to identify. The surface of the skin is rough and bumpy in appearance; it is heavily encrusted with organisms similar to the well-known barnacles that can be found clinging to reefs (though in this case they belong to a different species) and other parasitic crustaceans, which are responsible for the yellowish spots. Instead of a dorsal fin, there is a series of small humps, diminishing along the body all the way down to the tail. Along the belly, there are a number of grooves not unlike those found in humpback whales and fin whales, but fewer in number—from two to five. The gray whale has no close "relatives"; it is the only species in the Eschrichtiidae family, considered to be the most primitive family in the suborder of baleen whales. Its largely coastal habits—more so than any other whale—makes it the best known of whales.

Almost everything that is known about the gray whale was discovered by studying the population of the eastern Pacific, which in winter gathers in the lagoons of Baja California and in the summer can be found in the Bering Sea and the Beaufort Sea. A second "stock" of gray

whales, the Korean gray, lives in the western Pacific and is now on the verge of extinction, a fate that has already befallen the populations of the North Atlantic, wiped out by whalers in the seventeenth and eighteenth centuries. Because it tends to frequent closed bodies of water near the coast and tends to migrate along the coasts, the gray whale was one of the first species to be hunted by whalers. In 1880, it was considered to be "commercially" extinct. But once the whalers left it alone, it recovered in numbers. It was hunted once again until 1937 when, for the second time, the population was reduced to a minimum. From 1946 on, the species has been protected from commercial hunting. Whalers dubbed these whales "devilfish." The reason was that when the whalers harpooned the young to make sure that the mother whale would stay within harpooning distance, she would sometimes attack the whaler's boats. Today, however, gray whales have proved to be the whales that are most sociable toward humans. In the lagoons of Baja California, they have been accustomed for years to the approach of visitors and at times can even be touched.

The migration of the gray whale is the longest that a mammal has been observed to make; in one year a gray whale will swim no fewer than 12,500 miles in its round trip journey from winter grounds to summer grounds and back again. This species spends its summer in the chilly but food-rich waters of the arctic seas and its winter in the warmer regions such as the lagoons of Baja California. In the north, the whales eat their fill of the small crustaceans on the seabed, while once they have moved south, they forego eating almost entirely and instead devote themselves to mating and to raising their young. This organization, over the course of a year, is typical of almost all the baleen whales; indeed, the humpbacks, the right whales, and, to a lesser degree, the rorquals, all do the same thing. They are capable of more or less fasting for eight months, and then they gulp down nearly all of their yearly food requirements in the few remaining weeks. And one should consider that the females have to face the challenge—not a slight one, in terms of energy consumption—of suckling their young. They give birth after arriving in the summer grounds, around January. In March, the females take the young with them as they start off north again, constantly providing them with vast quantities of extremely rich milk

Gray whales, especially the females, which are larger than the males, can attain weights up to 37 tons, the equivalent of five African elephants. This is still small compared to the blue whale, the largest animal on earth, whose maximum weight is equal to that of 25 elephants.

and it is not until May, when they reach the arctic, that they can begin to eat once again.

One might well wonder just why they accept this difficult routine. The explanation, perhaps, is that the young cannot face the chilly waters of the north and must be born in the tepid waters of the south. When they are born, they lack the thick insulated layer of blubber that will protect them from the chill as they grow. But the southern climes do not supply the whales with enough food, and so they must periodically go in search of nourishment in the rich polar waters. There are, however, much smaller cetaceans (which are therefore more exposed to the cold) that encounter no difficulties in being born in very cold waters.

Gray whales, therefore, would theoretically have no trouble at all doing the same; it may be that they migrate for other reasons. Baleen whales might well have originated in warm waters, where there might have been plenty of food at the time. But that food supply might eventually have dried up, the prey moving elsewhere. The cetaceans, in this case, might have begun migrating north periodically in search of their favorite crustaceans and finally have reached the arctic, in the areas they now habitually haunt. They would still have continued to return—by "habit"—to their old mating grounds.

Whatever the case, migration profoundly conditions the behavior and biology of these whales. For example, because of the migration, the female gray whales are generally much larger

The gray whale's baleen, or whalebone, the fibrous plates hanging from the palate and used to filter food, is relatively short, measuring from two to ten inches in length. The longest are those of the bow-head whale, ranging up to four yards long.

than the males, since they have to store enough fat to suckle their young for seven months. Moreover, when the time comes to migrate, the females who have just conceived are always in a rush; during the northward migration, they move quickly to the feeding areas, probably in order to have more time to eat. The adult males and young males and females follow at a more leisurely pace. In the subsequent southward migration, as well, the pregnant females tend to set off first, in a hurry to reach the south in plenty of time to bear their young. This happens, for each female, no more frequently than every two years. The cycle works as follows—during the winter, around the beginning of December, the whales mate just before they reach the lagoons, and the following winter the little whale is born (the period of gestation is just over a year). It is not until the following winter, when the young whale no longer suckles, that the female is again available for reproduction. Therefore, each female whale can produce offspring only every two years. This has a great influence on the biology of cetaceans, with their very low rate of reproduction. Whale populations subjected to the decimation of whalers soon dwindle to the point of extinction because they cannot quickly replenish the lost individuals. Moreover, a gray whale is not old enough to reproduce until the age of eight, making the survival of these cetaceans just that much more fragile.

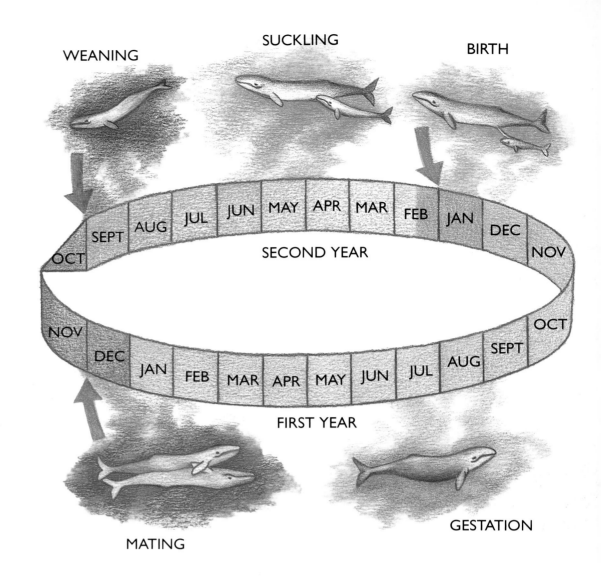

BOTTOM-FEEDING MANEUVER OF THE GRAY WHALE

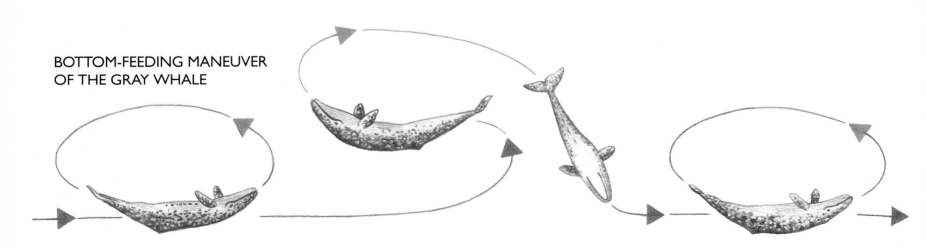

FEEDING IN THE MUD

Although they eat by filtration like all the other baleen whales, gray whales obtain nourishment in a remarkable manner. Indeed, they do not go in search of plankton floating in the water, but rather they eat animals that live on the seabed. From June to October, they graze in this way, which involves diving to the shallower bottoms (16 to 330 feet), rolling over on one side, and then swimming slowly along, their mouths just grazing the sea floor, sucking in mud and food. Then, as they return to the surface, they expel the mud, leaving a yellowish trail behind them, and they keep everything that is edible in the

great mouthful they have just taken. For the most part, that means krill, other isopods, sea worms, and mollusks. As they do this, the gray whales dig great trenches as they go, literally plowing the sea floor. At first glance, one might suppose that this sort of activity, when practiced by a great many whales, might wind up throwing the environment of the sea floor into chaos, causing all sorts of damage, especially if we consider that each of the swaths that a feeding gray whale cuts across the sea floor can be from 10 to 350 square feet. This is probably not the case, however, and indeed this excavation probably

serves to increase the productivity of the zone. A few years ago, a group of researchers made an effort to verify this theory of "seabed plowing." Just off the island of Vancouver, Canada, where a small group of gray whales feed during the summer, they produced artificial trenches not unlike those produced by the cetaceans. After a while, they observed that new crustaceans had come to inhabit the seabed. Moreover, they were prospering even more than those in the area not plowed.

BLUE WHALE
Balaenoptera musculus

AVERAGE SIZE

Newborns:	23 feet
Adults:	(females) 85 feet
	(males) 82 feet
Weight:	88-145 tons

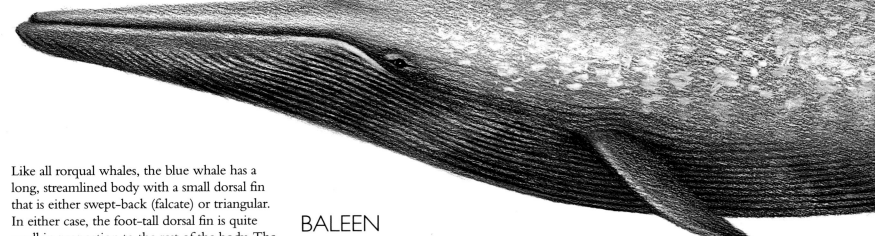

Like all rorqual whales, the blue whale has a long, streamlined body with a small dorsal fin that is either swept-back (falcate) or triangular. In either case, the foot-tall dorsal fin is quite small in proportion to the rest of the body. The body is smooth, with small, light-colored patches, and the grayish coloration may have a slight bluish tint, hence the name. The head, when seen from above, is U-shaped, and it is divided lengthwise by a central crest that runs from the tip of the snout to the blowholes. There are about 60 longitudinal grooves along the belly and throat, and they stretch a little over halfway along the body. Like all rorquals, the blue whale is a fast swimmer, and normally cruises at about 3-4 knots (3.5-4.6 miles per hour).

Blue whales can be found in almost all of the oceans in the world, but there are three major populations—found in the northern Pacific, the northern Atlantic, and throughout the southern hemisphere. The latter population, following the classic pattern of the baleen whales, spend the summer in the krill-rich waters of the Antarctic and then migrate toward warmer waters such as those off Brazil, Ecuador, South Africa, and—less frequently—Australia and New Zealand.

Because of the remarkable quantities of blubber and flesh that they yield, blue whales have long been the preferred prey of industrial whalers. The result has been a sharp dwindling of the population everywhere, even though blue whales have been a protected species since 1965. As of this writing, blue whales have given no sign of recovering their numbers. Of the 5,000 that were probably alive in the Pacific Ocean before commercial whaling began, slightly fewer than 1,000 survived, according to estimates; and in the Antarctic, of the 250,000 present in the nineteenth century, there are perhaps 9,000 survivors, and half of those belong to a pygmy subspecies (*Balaenoptera musculus brevicauda*).

BALEEN

Although baleen, or whalebone, is useful in feeding, it is completely different from teeth; it could be more closely compared to our fingernails. Whalebones are usually thick plates, broad and compact at the base; toward the tips they tend to become thin and fringed. They grow directly from the tissues of the palate (the ridges that dogs have in the roofs of their mouths correspond more or less to the part of the whale's palate that "generates" whalebone). When the baleen whale is ready to eat, water flows into the mouth and the whale's tongue acts as a giant piston, pushing liquid out, while the baleen captures the food—small fish or plankton. This is the fundamental technique, but there are variations. Indeed, filtering cetaceans have various specializations and occupy various environmental niches that could correspond, say, to those of herbivores on the savannah. Although zebras, gazelles, and giraffes all survive in the same environment, each has specialized in eating specific plants. Likewise, baleen whales each have established a niche of their own, distinguished by a specific feeding technique and a specific type of prey.

There are two major categories of filtering cetaceans, the "gulpers" and the "skimmers." The first category includes the rorquals and the humpback whale. Their strategy is limited to filling their mouths with enormous quantities of water; the longitudinal grooves along the belly and throat stretch like an accordion, accommodating the added bulk of water. The water is then expelled from the sides of the mouth and the plankton is retained and swallowed. The right whales, on the other hand, are skimmers; they filter chiefly on the surface, swimming along with their mouths open; the water thus passes directly through the filtering apparatus. The whalebones of the bowhead whale are the longest of all whalebones, having been measured at over 13 feet in length (they were once the source of the famous whalebone corsets). They fill the whale's mouth, which is equal to one-third of the whale's total length. The mouth is also quite high, as the upper bones of the rostrum form an enormous arch. The consistency of the baleen can also vary, depending on the chosen prey. The baleen of the right whales are flexible and tend to fringe in very fine "hairs," perfect for trapping tiny animals such as the larvae of krill. Rorqual whales, on the other hand, have relatively short whalebones (those found in the giant blue whale measure "only" three feet in length by twenty inches in width) and are perfectly suited for filtering krill. The fin whales have larger fringes and eat shrimp but also larger prey such as small schooling fish. The "midget" of rorqual whales is the minke whale—its whalebones are no longer than seven inches and only three inches wide.

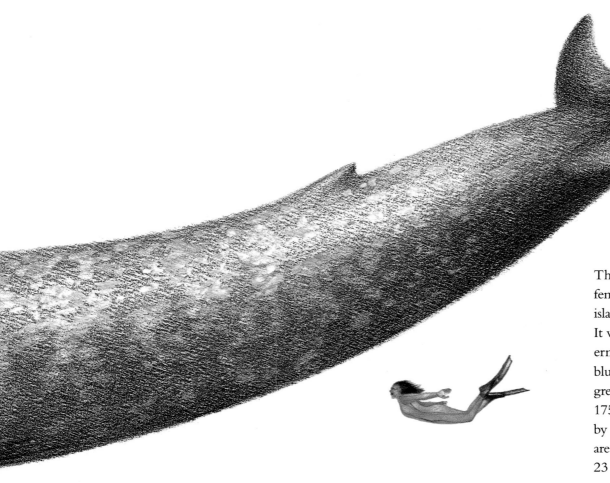

The largest blue whale ever measured was a female brought in to the whaling station on an island off Cape Horn at the turn of the century. It was 110 feet long, slightly smaller than a modern DC-9 airplane. Record specimens aside, the blue whales of the southern hemisphere often grew to 100 feet in length, weighing as much as 175 tons before the largest ones were killed off by whaling. The blue whales of modern times are generally smaller, but they still measure about 23 feet in length at birth. Little blue whales grow at an astonishing rate: they put on nearly 200 pounds a day, thanks to the 50 gallons or so of milk, extremely rich in fats, the mother whale provides daily. Paradoxically, this animal—the largest that has ever lived on earth—lives on tiny shrimp. During the feeding season in the Antarctic, each blue whale gulps down four-and-a-half tons daily—about four million of the little animals. It is calculated that in some cases, the daily "ration" of a blue whale can amount to almost nine tons of food. For comparison, the smaller baleen whales are the minke whales, which grow to 33 feet in length, and the pygmy right whales, which do not grow any longer than 20 feet. Among the toothed whales, the largest is the sperm whale (which can grow as long as 60 feet). The sperm whale holds two other records—it possesses the largest brain in the animal kingdom (20 pounds) and it is the largest living active predator. The smallest cetaceans are the Cephalorhynchae, four species of the dolphin family; they generally are no bigger than six feet in length. In the populations found off the South American coast, the male adult Commerson's dolphin is only four to five feet in length.

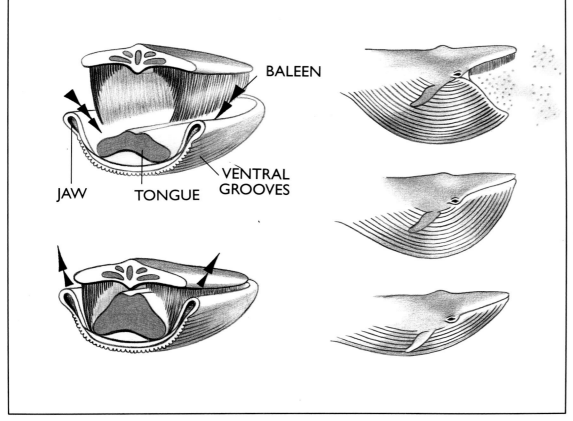

**BALEEN STRUCTURE AND
FEEDING METHOD OF THE BLUE WHALE**

RIGHT WHALE

Eubalaena glacialis,
Eubalaena australis

AVERAGE SIZE

Newborns:	15-20 feet
Adults:	(females) 60 feet
	(males) 50 feet
Weight:	66-110 tons

There are two kinds of right whale—the northern (Eubalaena glacialis) and the southern (Eubalaena australis), but the actual differences between the two types are minimal. There are a number of scientists who feel that there should be no distinction between the two. Right whales, although not as long as the rorqual whales, are far more rotund and completely devoid of dorsal fins. Their heads are very large and the upper mandible is narrow and arches slightly upward. The enormous lower lip serves to close the mouth, with its long whalebone plates at the sides. At the tip of the snout and above the eyes are whitish calluses that stand out

against the rest of the very dark body. There is another of these calluses at the top of the head, eloquently called a "bonnet." The presence of these calluses, infested as they are with parasites, makes it possible to distinguish between the right whale and the bowhead whale, which is similar but is free of these encrustations. The pectoral flippers are triangular, large, and quite different from the streamlined flippers of the rorquals.

Right whales are relatively slow swimmers, and only over brief stretches can they reach speeds of 6.5 knots (7.5 miles per hour). That is one of the reasons they fell easy prey to

the eighteenth- and nineteenth-century whalers, who killed them by the tens of thousands. The other "advantages" of right whales were the enormous quantities of oil and blubber that they would yield and their fondness for coastal waters. In a short span of time, right whales dwindled from great populations to the brink of extinction. And there they remain, even today, although they have not been hunted since 1937. The estimates for the populations of the Atlantic and the Pacific indicate a few hundred whales; in the southern hemisphere, where the numbers are finally beginning to increase, there are probably a couple of thousand.

WHALE-WATCHING

If whales were depicted for centuries as horrible monsters, one of the reasons may have been that to see one in the flesh was the privilege of only a few mariners and adventurers. Only in the past few years have "dry-landers" been able to encounter gray or fin whales just by hopping on a boat and taking a ride. Whale-watching is becoming increasingly popular. This type of ecotourism was invented in the U.S. but is expanding throughout the rest of the world as fast as new areas frequented regularly by dolphins or whales can be discovered. The image of whales in the collective imagination has changed radically—instead of being considered leviathans, they are now thought of as gentle giants, harmless creatures that have no interest in attacking boats or humans that mean them no harm. This applies to right whales, which were once hunted down and slaughtered by whalers but are now tourist attractions off the Valdés Peninsula in Argentina, where the southern right whales gather from July to November. Equal "celebrities" are the gray whales, which can be seen in the winter in the Pacific Ocean lagoons of Baja California. These large cetaceans allow humans in rubber dinghies to approach them, and at times the young whales will swim up to humans, sticking their heads curiously out of the water. The history of whale-watching began with this species a little further north, in California proper. There, during the fifties, researchers had begun to study passing whales during their long migration. The first pleasure seekers interested in watching whales appeared in San Diego. Today, a great many localities boast of whales and dolphins among their tourist attractions. A distant corner of British Columbia, Ucluelet on the island of Vancouver, has even proclaimed itself to be the "world capital of whale-watching." In the summer, two small groups—one of gray whales and one of humpback whales—stop just off the coast and can be reached in a boat trip of just a few hours. On the other side of the island, there are other cetaceans, better known among whale-watchers—killer whales, which can be easily spotted during the summer months in the strait that separates the island of Vancouver from the continent, and in Puget Sound, just across the American border. Also popular are the humpbacks that winter just off the Hawaiian Islands and those that can be seen off Cape Cod. In Europe, too, whale-watching is catching on. For example, in Scotland, an area frequented by minke whales has been found off the island of Mull in the Hebrides; and in the Ligurian Sea, off Italy, research cruises are organized regularly, and are open to the public interested in seeing fin whales. Some scientists fear that the presence of too many boats, especially in the mating areas, can disturb the animals, further endangering the species. Some countries, such as Canada and the United States, have introduced regulations governing how closely boats can approach the whales; it is hoped that this will provide some protection from that danger. On the other hand, the development of whale-watching has unquestionably helped to put a halt to the ruthless exploitation of whales, and it can be considered to some extent as a preferable alternative to whaling. In some countries, including the United States, eco-tourism is a growing industry, and it is probably safe to say that in America at least (unlike in countries like Norway, Iceland, and Japan, which still whale extensively), a live whale is valued more than a dead one.

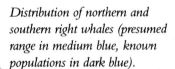

Distribution of northern and southern right whales (presumed range in medium blue, known populations in dark blue).

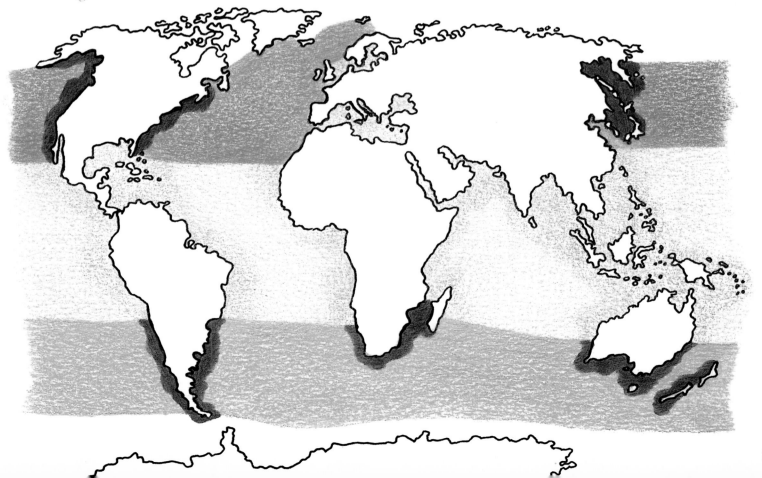

SPERM WHALE

Physeter catodon

AVERAGE SIZE

Newborns:	13 feet
Adults:	(males) 50-60 feet
	(females) 36 feet
Weight:	15-55 tons

The largest of all the toothed whales is dark in color with some white markings, mostly around the jaws; its body has wrinkled skin around the sides, and the dorsal fin is a sort of hump followed by a series of diminishing knobs along the midline. The tail, which towers over the surface of the water when the whale begins a dive, is triangular. At sea, it is possible to identify a sperm whale by its spray, which is "tilted" slightly forward because of the asymmetrical configuration of the nasal passages and the blowhole. Unlike baleen whales, among the sperm whales (and many other toothed whales), the males are larger than the females. The head, which constitutes a third of the animal's length, is large and has a square silhouette. This shape is chiefly due to the presence of the so-called "organ of spermaceti," a large sac containing a waxy substance which was once greatly prized as a lubricant. Its function is not clear; it may serve to counterbalance hydrodynamic thrust when the whale dives, or it could be a "lens" for biosonar (an acoustic detection system found in toothed whales, although it has not yet been established whether sperm whales also have biosonar). Certainly the spermaceti has nothing to do with sperm, though whalers once thought that the whale was full of the substance. Hidden by the enormous bulk of the head, the lower jaw is surprisingly narrow and long; it contains a series of

conical teeth. These teeth are the reason that the sperm whale is considered to be closer to dolphins than to other whales. There are two other, smaller "relatives" in the same family Physeteridae—the pygmy sperm whale and the dwarf sperm whale. Except during the mating season, which occurs in winter in the warm regions, the groups of male sperm whales tend to live separately from those of females with their young; in the summer, the males migrate toward subpolar waters, while the females and young tend to remain in temperate climes. Whalers began to hunt sperm whales in the eighteenth century, but modern industrial hunting in the sixties began to decimate the numbers of certain populations. Despite this wholesale slaughter, there are still a fair number of sperm whales around the world. Some estimates place that number around 1.5 million; others say that there are no more than 500,000 still alive.

RECORD DIVES

The sperm whale is capable of staying under water for remarkably long periods of time, and these performances require equally remarkable physiological adaptations. The "technical adaptations" required are fundamentally the same in all cetaceans, but since they have been developed to their most spectacular form in the sperm whale, let's follow one during a dive. After taking a series of breaths on the surface, the sperm whale raises its triangular tail and begins to dive

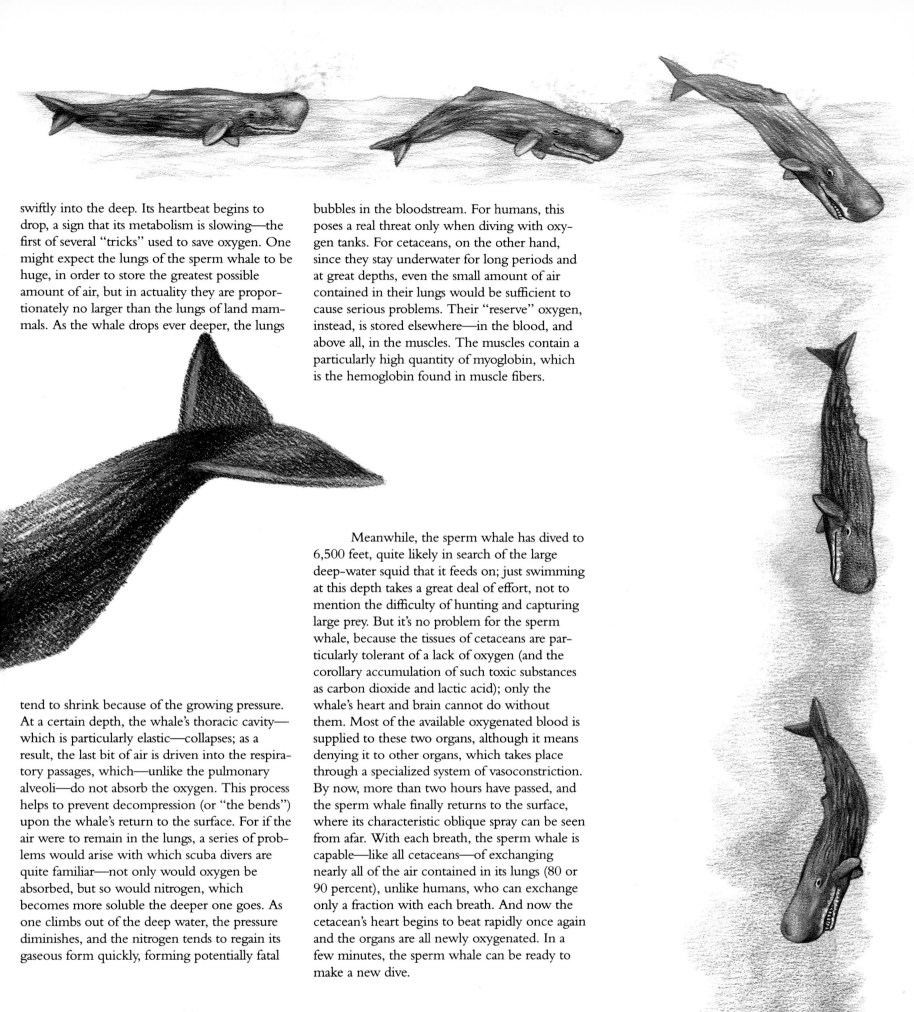

swiftly into the deep. Its heartbeat begins to drop, a sign that its metabolism is slowing—the first of several "tricks" used to save oxygen. One might expect the lungs of the sperm whale to be huge, in order to store the greatest possible amount of air, but in actuality they are proportionately no larger than the lungs of land mammals. As the whale drops ever deeper, the lungs

tend to shrink because of the growing pressure. At a certain depth, the whale's thoracic cavity—which is particularly elastic—collapses; as a result, the last bit of air is driven into the respiratory passages, which—unlike the pulmonary alveoli—do not absorb the oxygen. This process helps to prevent decompression (or "the bends") upon the whale's return to the surface. For if the air were to remain in the lungs, a series of problems would arise with which scuba divers are quite familiar—not only would oxygen be absorbed, but so would nitrogen, which becomes more soluble the deeper one goes. As one climbs out of the deep water, the pressure diminishes, and the nitrogen tends to regain its gaseous form quickly, forming potentially fatal

bubbles in the bloodstream. For humans, this poses a real threat only when diving with oxygen tanks. For cetaceans, on the other hand, since they stay underwater for long periods and at great depths, even the small amount of air contained in their lungs would be sufficient to cause serious problems. Their "reserve" oxygen, instead, is stored elsewhere—in the blood, and above all, in the muscles. The muscles contain a particularly high quantity of myoglobin, which is the hemoglobin found in muscle fibers.

Meanwhile, the sperm whale has dived to 6,500 feet, quite likely in search of the large deep-water squid that it feeds on; just swimming at this depth takes a great deal of effort, not to mention the difficulty of hunting and capturing large prey. But it's no problem for the sperm whale, because the tissues of cetaceans are particularly tolerant of a lack of oxygen (and the corollary accumulation of such toxic substances as carbon dioxide and lactic acid); only the whale's heart and brain cannot do without them. Most of the available oxygenated blood is supplied to these two organs, although it means denying it to other organs, which takes place through a specialized system of vasoconstriction. By now, more than two hours have passed, and the sperm whale finally returns to the surface, where its characteristic oblique spray can be seen from afar. With each breath, the sperm whale is capable—like all cetaceans—of exchanging nearly all of the air contained in its lungs (80 or 90 percent), unlike humans, who can exchange only a fraction with each breath. And now the cetacean's heart begins to beat rapidly once again and the organs are all newly oxygenated. In a few minutes, the sperm whale can be ready to make a new dive.

NARWHAL
Monodon monoceros

AVERAGE SIZE

Newborns:	5 feet
Adults:	(males) 13-16 feet (*excluding tusk*)
	(females) 11.5-13 feet
Weight:	up to 3,500 lbs.

Even if they seem like outsized dolphins with densely spotted black-and-white skins, narwhals do not actually belong to the family Delphinidae, but to the family Mondontidae, along with the beluga. The narwhal's color changes during the course of its life; at birth, the young are gray or bluish-gray, and they darken as they grow until they become practically black. When they reach maturity, light-colored spots begin to appear, gradually increasing in number and extension; fully-grown or aged specimens—especially males—may be entirely white. The narwhal's tail has an unusual shape—a "fantail"—while the tips of the pectoral fins tend to tilt somewhat upwards. The long tusk that distinguishes male narwhals may often be visible when they surface; aside from the tusk, when a narwhal surfaces, little is visible besides the back, which is devoid of a dorsal fin. This species lives exclusively in arctic waters, and in particular in Baffin Bay just off the coasts of Greenland, and in Davis Strait. Small populations can be found

in Canada's Hudson Bay and Hudson Strait and in the Barents Sea. Narwhals tend to prefer the areas around the icepack; their seasonal migrations are therefore dependent on icepack formation. In the summer, they tend to move northward, keeping close to the main pack and to icefloes; for this reason, in the fall, it is not uncommon for a number of animals, straggling behind the main migration, to die trapped in the ice. Traditionally, narwhals are the prey of native "subsistence hunters." There is, moreover, a certain market for the long, spiraled ivory tusks. There are no reliable estimates of the total number of narwhals, save for the largest single population, which can be found during the summer in Lancaster Sound, Canada; this population is believed to count some 20,000 individuals.

A single tusk, up to 10 feet long and weighing about 20 pounds, jutting from the narwhal's snout, must be a fairly cumbersome adornment to carry about. And yet male narwhals have survived for millions of years with

this strange decoration provided by nature. Science has not yet provided a definitive explanation of the function of this enormous tusk.

Narwhals have only two teeth, located in the upper part of the mouth; these teeth remain hidden in female and young narwhals, while in the mature males, the left tusk begins to develop disproportionately into a long and twisted tusk. The tusk can be over eight inches in diameter at the base. It extends forward and a little downward. Its spiral structure (which twists counter-clockwise) may serve to reduce the hydrodynamic resistance as the narwhal swims; this is one of the many hypotheses that have been advanced to explain this strange appendage. As for the efforts to attribute a function to the tusk itself, one could fill a book. It was originally thought that the tusk might serve to force passages through the blocks of the icepack, thus allowing the narwhal to cut itself breathing holes. Then it was thought that it could serve to help the whale pick through the seabed in search of crabs and other small morsels, or even to run through the fish that might be too large to fit into the narwhal's mouth. Other theories refer to the possibility that the tusk was used a defense against predators, as a support when resting upon the ice, as a sort of antenna for the transmission and reception of sounds, or even as a heat-regulating structure.

None of these hypotheses, however, was entirely sound, for the simple reason that if the tusk were used to procure food or for other functions of vital importance, it was not clear how the females and young could do without it. The most logical interpretation was that the tusk constituted a secondary sexual attribute—like the coxcombs of roosters or the manes of lions. It could, in other words, be nothing more than a narwhal's way of showing off its masculinity, or it might serve as a weapon in the duels between males for the conquest of females.

In reality, too little is known of this species that haunts the most distant waters of the Arctic to say whether it is disposed to duels of this sort, and whether there exists a hierarchy, and just how relations between adults are sorted out. In any case, a number of factors support the idea that the tusk has a "military" use—males have

been observed more than once "crossing" their tusks on the surface like fencers *en garde*. Moreover, among the tusks recovered by hunters, one out of three has the tip broken off. This is not all—the bodies and heads of male narwhals, unlike those of females, are often marked by scars. Last of all, the tip is usually polished and abraded, unlike the base, which is covered with algae—a sign that in one way or another, the mysterious tusk is used on a regular basis.

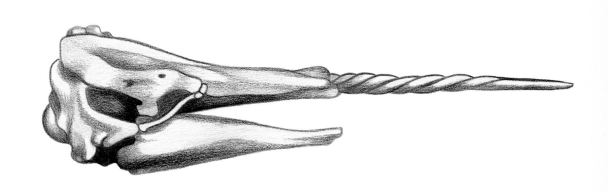

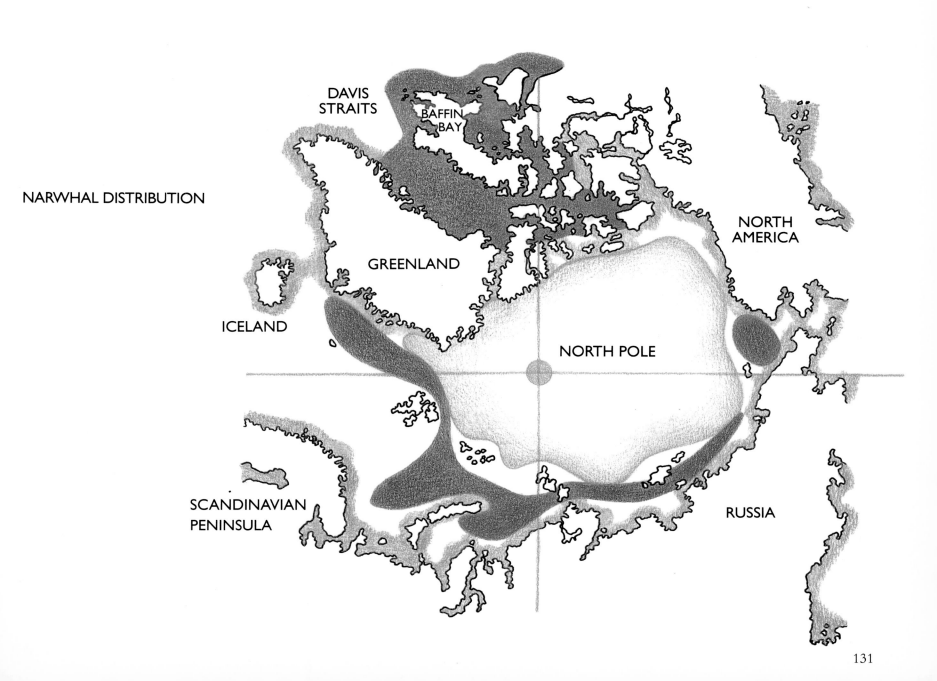

NARWHAL DISTRIBUTION

DAVIS STRAITS

BAFFIN BAY

GREENLAND

NORTH AMERICA

ICELAND

NORTH POLE

SCANDINAVIAN PENINSULA

RUSSIA

BELUGA
Delphinapterus leucas

AVERAGE SIZE

Newborns:	5 feet
Adults:	(males) 15 feet
	(females) 12 feet
Weight:	up to 3,300 pounds

In the illustration below, a newborn and a young whale are shown with a female to indicate color development. Like all cetaceans, beluga bear only one offspring at a time.

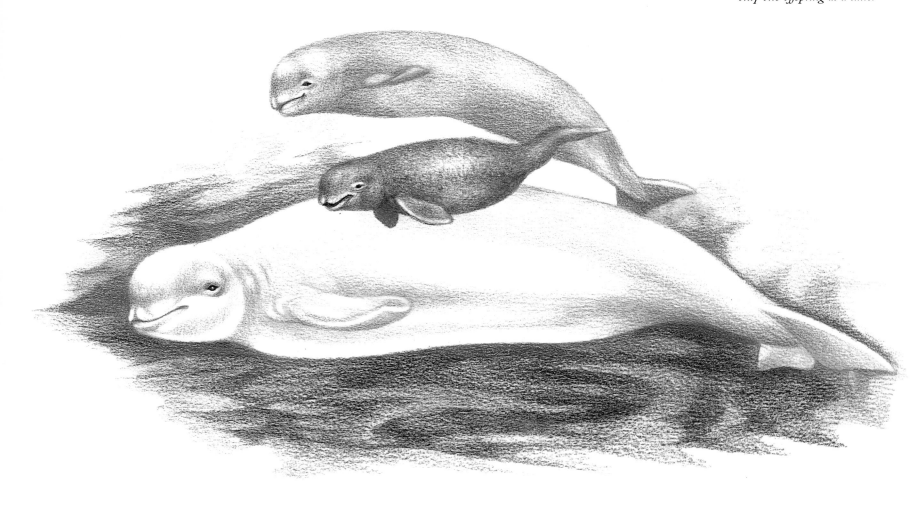

Like narwhals, belugas live only in the cold arctic seas. Their coloration depends on their age—the light gray of the newborn beluga is transformed into a bluish tint in young belugas, and it is not until the age of six or seven, when maturity is attained, that belugas take on the distinctive creamy white coloring of adulthood. The head and the pectoral fins are small in comparison with the body, and in the place where one might expect to find a dorsal fin there is just a fold of skin, slightly darker in color. Unlike all the other cetaceans, the beluga enjoys a certain mobility of the neck, which means that it can rotate its head, and—another unusual feature—it boasts a series of facial expressions. The latter detail suggests that belugas have a complex social life. For that matter, belugas also boast a remarkable vocal repertoire, including a broad range of whistles, squeaks, rumbles, and grunts. Besides those sounds, there are also the "clicks" of their biosonar (a sort of echolocation system specific to toothed whales) and the occasional, thunderous slamming of the jaws. At times, such sounds are so intense that they can be heard even by

someone out of the water. These combined vocal "talents" have earned the belugas the nickname "canaries of the sea." The meaning of all these forms of communication is not entirely clear, just as little is known about the internal organization of the pods. In any case, as is common among the toothed whales, the females and the young tend to separate from the groups of males. Belugas were hunted in the eighteenth and nineteenth centuries, and they still are, to some extent, by the native peoples of the north. Nowadays, however, belugas are in greater danger from the changes in their habitat than from anything else. Many populations have dwindled—for instance, the belugas of the Saint Lawrence River, in southeast Canada, are no more than 500 in number. In Lancaster Sound, on the other hand, further north, a fair number still survive—about 10,000, while another 11,000 are found in the western part of the Hudson Bay and Hudson Strait. The world population is estimated to be somewhere between 26,000 and 70,000.

Belugas usually live in small groups of 10 or 20 whales, scattered all over the farthest reaches of the Arctic. Once a year, however, in the summer, they gather by the thousands in specific bays and near the mouths of rivers in northern Canada. In the delta of the Mackenzie River along the far northern coast of the American continent, up to 5,000 belugas gather in July and August. In all likelihood, they come from the Bering Sea, where they pass the winter; when the ice begins to melt, they head north, passing the Bering Strait which separates Alaska from Siberia and, following the U.S. coast, they reach their summer quarters. Then, in September, when the icepack begins to form, they return southward along the same route. In Hudson Bay, as well, on the eastern coast of Canada, belugas gather in much the same way. In the mouths of the Nelson, Churchill, and Seal Rivers, a total of some 6,500 belugas gather in July. The same thing happens on Somerset Island off northern Canada, where some 5,000-5,500 belugas converge in Creswell Bay and Cunningham Bay. The reason for these

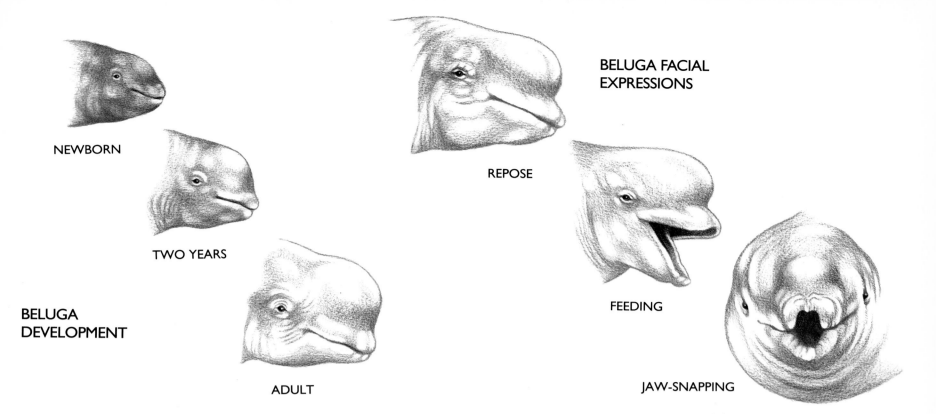

BELUGA DEVELOPMENT

NEWBORN

TWO YEARS

ADULT

BELUGA FACIAL EXPRESSIONS

REPOSE

FEEDING

JAW-SNAPPING

spectacular gatherings is still being studied by researchers. Above all, the habit can prove to be very dangerous to the belugas; in the past, hunters have driven panic-stricken belugas in great numbers onto the shore, where they have then slaughtered the whales at their leisure. A number of different hypotheses have been advanced to explain the gatherings. One idea is that the areas chosen are particularly advantageous for the birth of the young belugas—beluga females give birth in precisely this period. At the mouths of the rivers, the waters are warm, with temperatures ranging from 45 to 65 degrees Fahrenheit, while the surrounding seas are at freezing or barely above. This could be a very important factor for the newborn whales, which have very little insulating blubber. In reality, however, mother whales have been sighted swimming with newborns in very cold water, which leads one to suppose that the birth of the

young cannot be the only reason for these vast congregations of belugas, especially as both males and immature females take part in the gatherings. One might then suppose that these gatherings are mating rendezvous. But we can discard this hypothesis as well, since gestation lasts fourteen months and the young are therefore conceived prior to the summer. Another idea that has been considered is that the gatherings could be related to food. Belugas have a varied diet comprised of fish, cephalopods, and crustaceans, and they could be attracted to river deltas by the abundance of food to be found there. However, thus far no evidence has emerged to support this theory; indeed, the few specimens captured or found dead during the gatherings have empty stomachs. Moreover, the fact that belugas head out into the open sea periodically during the gatherings suggests that is when they feed. Yet another possibility is that

they favor enclosed waters because they feel that they are safe from predators such as killer whales or even polar bears. Gathering in a large group ensures a certain protection, which is particularly helpful when the young are being born.

A final, possible explanation has been advanced by researchers studying the belugas along the banks of the Cunningham River. One of the activities in which belugas have been seen to engage during the period of the gatherings is to rub themselves vigorously against the gravel and pebbles of the river beds. After a few days of this sort of activity, their skins—at first yellowish and infested with parasites—become clean and white. Perhaps the belugas come to the river mouths to clean their skins. A definitive explanation has not yet been provided. Perhaps what drives them, year after year, to gather in certain places, is a combination of these reasons, or some other reason we cannot yet imagine.

BELUGA DISTRIBUTION

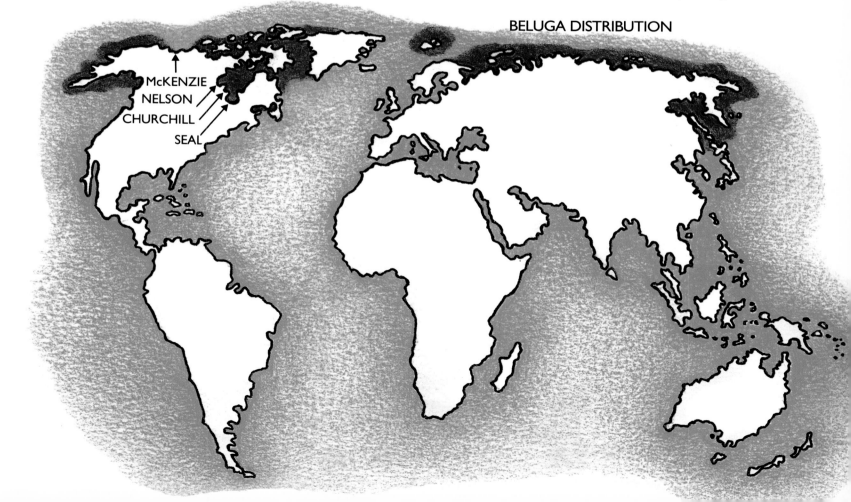

McKENZIE

NELSON

CHURCHILL

SEAL

KILLER WHALE
Orcinus orca

AVERAGE SIZE

Newborns:	7 feet
Adults:	(males) 30 feet
	(females) 20 feet
Weight:	(males) 9 tons
	(females) 4.5 tons

A large black-and-white spotted pattern makes it easy to identify this distinctive cetacean. Adult male killer whales have a triangular dorsal fin that can stand up to six feet tall, while the fin found on females and the young of both sexes is smaller and curved, similar in proportions to those found in other members of the family Delphinidae (the family to which *Orcinus orca* belongs). The unusually large and rounded pectoral fins are another distinctive feature of the killer whale. This is a wide-ranging species, found in all latitudes from warm seas to polar seas. The killer whale has never been actively hunted and is not currently considered to be an endangered species; killer whales are often killed by fishermen, especially by Icelandic and Norwegian fishermen, who consider them to be harmful to their catches. A number of individuals have been caught for dolphin shows, especially in recent decades, thus causing the population along the Pacific coasts to dwindle. Today, there is increasing debate over the display of killer whales in captivity. At the outset, however, the possibility of seeing these charming and spectacular animals in the flesh helped greatly to make the public more sensitive to issues concerning cetaceans and their environment.

The killer whales that live in the waters between the island of Vancouver and the western coast of Canada and the United States are the best-known community of cetaceans in the world. Researchers have been studying these large black-and-white Delphinidae for over 20 years, helped by the fact that these animals reside permanently, as it were, in a clearly circumscribed area, and that they can be individually recognized with a certain ease. The studies done to date have turned up some surprises. Killer whales have a social organization that is different from those of all the other cetaceans, since they live in particular family groups referred to as *pods*. In Johnstone Strait in the northern part of the island of Vancouver, there are twelve pods, while three others live to the south, extending all the way down to Puget Sound. The two communities, with a total population of about 250 killer whales, are "faithful" to their areas all year round, although killer whales are sighted more frequently in the summer and autumn. While most toothed whales tend to form into groups of males separate from the groups of females and young, killer whales—whether they are female or male—stay in the pod to which their mother belonged for the rest of their lives,

which can be as long as 68 years. The mothers and offspring of whatever age are joined, in time, by the offspring of succeeding generations. As for the fathers, their contribution to the reproductive process is limited to occasionally mating with the females of other families, after which both male and female return to their maternal pod.

A pod generally ranges from a few individuals to a few dozen, and its makeup varies only through births and deaths. In certain cases, a large family can break up into two subpods, or else one family may temporarily join with other pods. One thing that is quite certain, however, is that the members of the family know each other on an individual basis. During the sixties, when the first dolphin shows were being set up, if an individual killer whale was captured, the rest of the pod often tried to stay as close as possible to their unfortunate relative. Probably, the members of different pods also recognize each other, since two pods that encounter each other tend to express greetings that follow a prescribed ritual.

Equally emblematic of the cohesion of the group is the fact that each pod "speaks" its own dialect, and it is possible to determine the pod to which a killer whale belongs by listening

A POD OF KILLER
WHALES IN REPOSE

to its vocalizations. Basically, in each pod the sounds that typify the species *Orcinus orca* are emitted with a specific "accent" which is handed down from generation to generation. The area around the island of Vancouver, however, is frequented by other killer whales with slightly different characteristics, which we can refer to as "transient" killer whales. There are about 80 individuals, split up into smaller groups, and they appear only sporadically, probably roving over a larger area. The most spectacular difference between "transients" and "residents" is found in their feeding habits. The transients do not hesitate to attack larger prey such as seals, seal lions, and even other cetaceans, in keeping with their reputations as "killer whales."

Today, the idea is spreading among the public that there is little about killer whales that can truly be considered evil. This is not only because the "resident" killer whales tend to procure their food in a far less bloody manner (they chiefly eat salmon), but also because it is widely perceived that it is unjust to attach a moral judgement to an animal, especially based on its food-procuring strategies. For that matter, it is probably the very tendency to feed on fair-sized prey that caused killer whales to develop the qualities of familiarity and loyalty that we so admire in their social structure. Indeed, the capture of large animals (killer whales at times will even attack baleen whales) requires reliable and secure cooperation. This is the reason why individual killer whales must know each other well and cooperate successfully. Cases have been observed, though no plausible explanations have been provided for them, in which killer whales have attacked boats. On the other hand, we do not know of killer whales' having attacked humans in the water. Hostilities between members of the same species are fairly infrequent; in brief, we have discovered that killer whales are not "killers" at all.

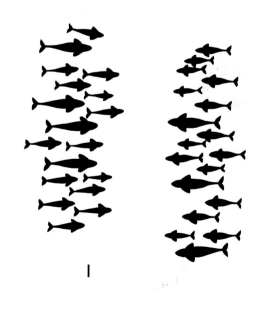

Two killer whale families meet (1), mingle (2), and break into smaller social groups (3).

1

2

3

BOTTLE-NOSED DOLPHIN
Tursiops truncatus

AVERAGE SIZE

Newborns:	3.5-4 feet
Adults:	8-9 feet
Weight:	up to 600 pounds

Probably the dolphin best known to the general public is the bottle-nosed dolphin, the variety most often found in marine parks, zoos, and circuses, and the star of the old television series "Flipper." The bottle-nosed dolphin's body is powerful, relatively squat, and features a large protruding beak that gives it its name. Its color is a uniform gray, varying in darkness, with a lighter belly. There are two different forms of this species—the coastal bottle-nosed dolphins, which tend to form small groups and at times reside in a specific area, and the "pelagic" bottle-nosed dolphins, which are found in the open sea in larger groups. There are no evident physical differences between the two forms, however, just as the males cannot be distinguished from the females at a glance. Bottle-nosed dolphins can be found more or less in all the seas of the world, except in the polar regions. From time to time, some particularly "inquisitive" or "friendly" member of the species approaches a beach or a marina and lets humans come close to it and even touch it.

There has been a great deal of discussion concerning the intelligence of dolphins, and a number of incidents of the rescue of shipwreck victims are mentioned as instances of the supposed exceptional capacities of different species.

In the sixties, the American scientist John Lilly attracted a great deal of attention by claiming that dolphins had capacities for abstract thought and comprehension that were equal to or even greater than those of human beings. Other researchers felt that Lilly's claims should be taken with a heaping teaspoon of salt. Lilly met with a very enthusiastic response, on the one hand, but was also roundly criticized for his vivisections of cetaceans and for administering drugs to them. He finally retired without ever having completely demonstrated his theories scientifically.

The debate over the intelligence of dolphins remains quite lively still. In reality, it would seem that the dolphins' predisposition to keep objects—and living things—afloat and in some cases to push them toward shore may derive more from particular instincts rather than from true, full-fledged "comprehension." However, "altruism" does play a fundamental role in dolphin biology. When a young dolphin is born, often the other females in the group help the mother to push the newborn toward the surface in order to allow it to take its first breath. Probably by an extension of the same form of behavior, dolphins feel impelled to help keep afloat an adult companion that is in some trouble. The same is true if the unfortunate "companion" found thrashing on the surface is a human being. Although it is very difficult to apply the concept of intelligence to animals suited to life in an environment so radically different from our own, there is plenty of evidence that justifies attributing intelligence to dolphins and other toothed whales. For example, they are animals that live on fish, which they have to capture actively, and this requires more intelligence than is needed by the larger, filtering cetaceans who literally swim through the plankton on which they feed.

Another indicator of intelligence is the ability to learn. Among the bottle-nosed dolphins, learning plays an important part in their life outside of captivity. Learning is involved in the recognition of individual companions, the boundaries of the family area, certain social rules, and, in all probability, methods of defense against predators, the techniques of echolocation, the capture of prey, and so on. It is for this reason that young dolphins spend a relatively long period with their mothers before setting out on an independent life of their own. Most of the real research intended to determine the degree of dolphin's intelligence, however, is conducted in the marine parks. The classic experiments are designed to determine whether cetaceans are capable of understanding abstract concepts. Until now, however, no one has succeeded in demonstrating that bottle-nosed dolphins are capable of communicating "abstract" messages among themselves. On the other hand, researchers have taught bottle-nosed dolphins to

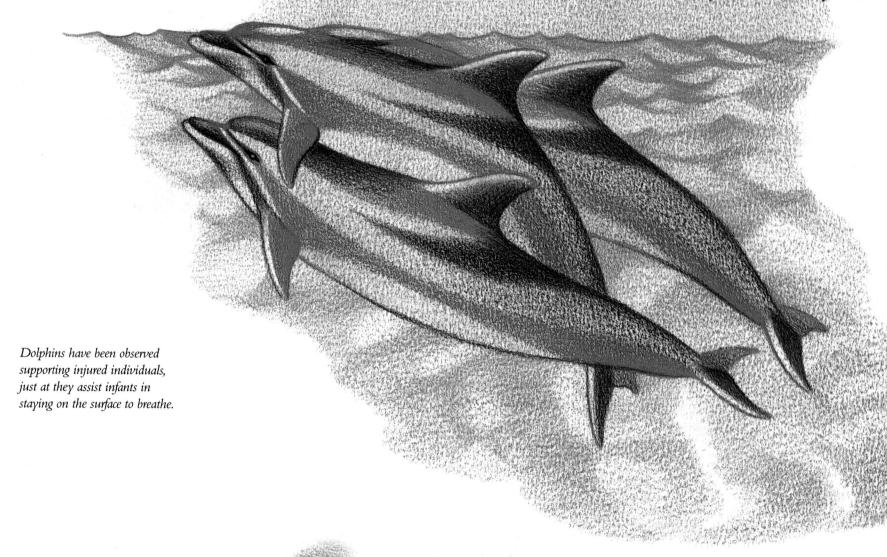

Dolphins have been observed supporting injured individuals, just at they assist infants in staying on the surface to breathe.

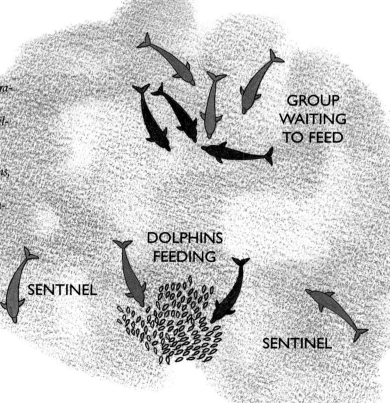

At times, dolphins feed cooperatively. Usually, they begin by surrounding fish so as to bewilder them and crowd them together. Then they begin to eat, in some cases, taking turns, as shown at right. Here, two dolphins feed, while two "sentinels" prevent the fish from scattering. The group at top looks on, awaiting their turn.

GROUP WAITING TO FEED

DOLPHINS FEEDING

SENTINEL

SENTINEL

associate a certain gesture or certain sounds with simple terms such as "ball," "circle," "cube," "carry," "seek," "left," and "right." In this way, the trainers can communicate with the animals, assembling sentences out of the various terms— "carry the ball," "seek the circle on the left," and so on. Many of the bottle-nosed dolphins trained in this way succeed in interpreting the orders correctly. But perhaps the most remarkable progress is that made by a female bottle-nose in a marine show in Hawaii. The trainer shows this dolphin a ball and asks her if it is a cylinder. She responds by pushing a lever, in this case, a lever that she has learned to associate with "no." And if what she is shown really is a cylinder, then she pushes a lever for "yes." What is most important, however, is that she does this for any type of cylinder that is shown to her, whether it is made out of plastic or steel and whether it is long, short, wide, or narrow. This leads us to suppose that this dolphin, at least, has succeeded in extrapolating an abstract concept— that of the geometric shape of an object. Other experiments with bottle-nosed dolphins are now being conducted in marine parks, some of them practically by accident. In California, one trainer taught the bottle-nosed dolphins to help clean out their tank. For every extraneous object that they brought the trainer, such as leaves, branches, or empty Coke cans, he would reward them with a fish. One of the female dolphins was particularly enthusiastic about this game and would bring him great numbers of pieces of paper, each time claiming the reward "promised." It was quite a while before the trainer realized that the dolphin was tricking him; she was bringing him pieces of paper that she would rip from a single paper bag that was hidden in a corner of the tank.

BOTTLE-NOSED DOLPHIN SOCIETY

Even though they have been observed closely for decades in captivity, we know relatively little about how dolphins live in the wild. Recently, however, methods have been devised for studying the animals in their natural state, and a number of stations have been set up for field work. In Europe, there is one in Croatia, where the researchers from the Tethys Institute of Milan, Italy, observe the bottle-nosed dolphins in the

waters off the islands of Cres and Cossinj. The longest-operating centers of research are found in Florida. The American studies have provided for the first time a variety of information about the life of a group of bottle-nosed dolphins. The group in question comprises about 100 individual bottle-nosed dolphins who live permanently in Sarasota Bay. What has emerged is an intriguing picture of the lives dolphins lead; of course, these observations do not apply to all the species of dolphins, but only to bottle-nosed dolphins, and in particular to those who frequent the coastal regions. Researchers are capable of distinguishing between various individuals by their markings, both artificial and natural (such as the notches that many bear on their dorsal fin), and can thus follow the events of their lives year after year—births, deaths, associations, types of activity. The dolphins of Sarasota Bay live in small groups, each of which seems to have favorite area. The groups are generally made up of either all males or all females with their young. The young bottle-nosed dolphins tend to remain

The birth of a dolphin. As soon as the infant emerges, it must take a breath, and if it cannot orient itself, the mother or other females in the group assist it in rising and staying on the surface.

with the group to which their mother belongs even after they have been weaned (which happens at the age of about a year), up to the age of three or four. After that age, they begin to spend more time with other adolescents, forming mixed groups, in which pre-adult males and females engage in lively activities of socialization. These activities include spectacular leaps, a vast range of vocalization, and games of all sorts. Once the bottle-nosed dolphins attain sexual maturity, the females return to the group into which they were born, while the males tend to form small, independent groups. Among the males, in the meanwhile, friendships have been formed; observations have been made of male individuals that spend large amounts of time

together. These special ties are probably destined to last for a bottle-nosed dolphin's lifetime; among other situations, it may happen that two "friends" court the same female and they may both manage to mate with the female without having this cause any friction between them, unlike what happens in analogous situations among other animals. As is the general rule among cetaceans, there are no lasting ties between males and females. The relationships are limited to mating, after which the female gives birth after a 12-month period of gestation. The lack of assistance from the males is made up for by the assistance of the other females in the group, who often help quite actively in caring for the young.

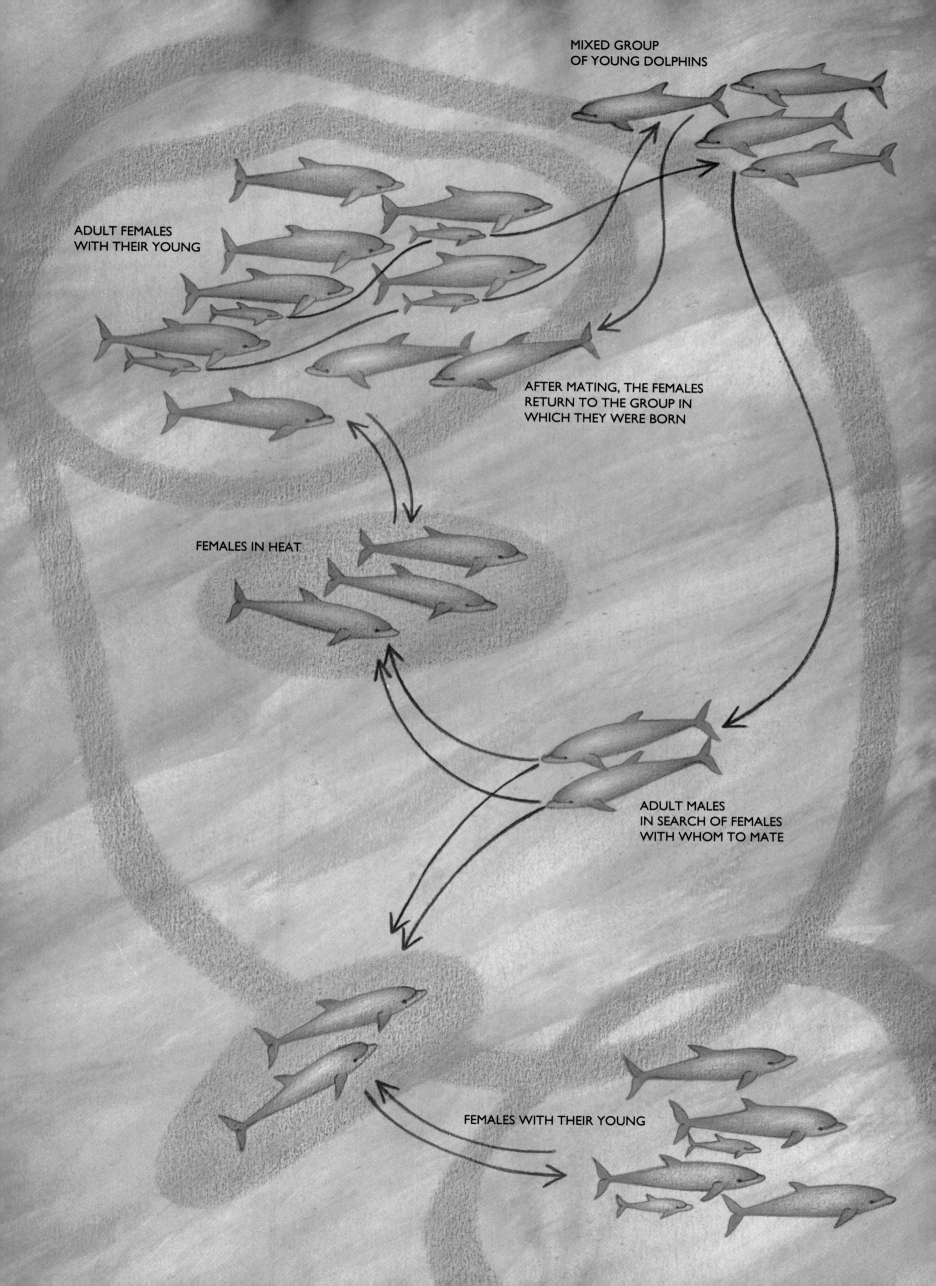

MIXED GROUP
OF YOUNG DOLPHINS

ADULT FEMALES
WITH THEIR YOUNG

AFTER MATING, THE FEMALES
RETURN TO THE GROUP IN
WHICH THEY WERE BORN

FEMALES IN HEAT

ADULT MALES
IN SEARCH OF FEMALES
WITH WHOM TO MATE

FEMALES WITH THEIR YOUNG

STRIPED DOLPHINS
Stenella coeruleoalba

AVERAGE SIZE

Newborns:	3.5 feet
Adults:	7.5-9 feet
Weight:	220 pounds

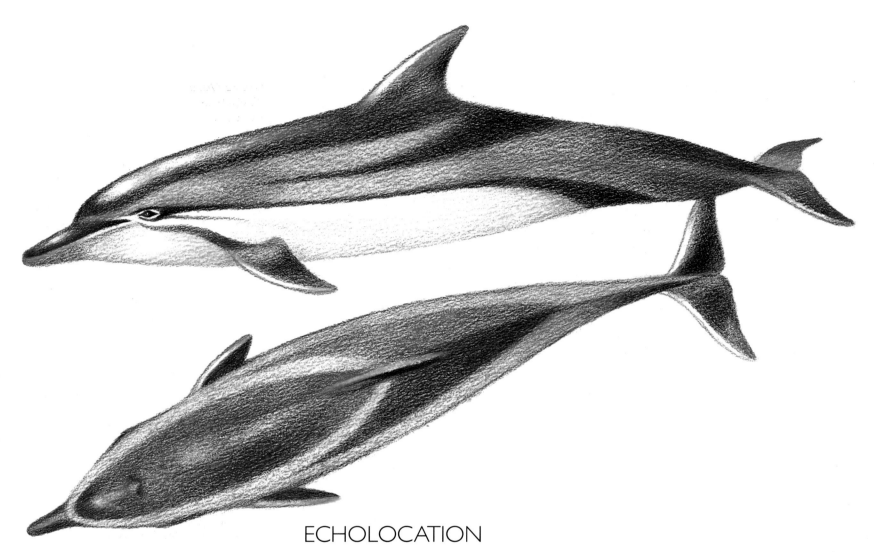

ECHOLOCATION

Striped dolphins are extremely elegant and graceful dolphins. Smaller and slimmer than the bottle-nosed dolphin, they are even more enthusiastic in their agile leaps out of the water, and they apparently enjoy bowriding with speedboats. Their coloration is fairly elaborate, with a series of light and dark stripes extending from their eyes and along their sides. They are distributed throughout the seas in temperate, tropical, and subtropical climes; in the Mediterranean, they represent the most common species. In the oceans, they often travel in large schools of several hundred, and, at times, even thousands of individuals. In the eastern Pacific, striped dolphins are among the species that, for reasons as yet unknown, swim with schools of tuna and therefore often become fatally entangled in the meshes of fishing trawlers, even though they are not the intended victims. The species as a whole is not considered to be endangered, although there are some fears for the survival of certain local populations such as those that are hunted along the coasts of Japan.

Modulated whistles, intense clicking noises, and sonorous clacks are all part of the vast range of sounds emitted by cetaceans. These animals make extensive use of acoustic communication, and this is no accident; in water, light penetrates feebly, unlike sound, which travels even better under water than it does in air. Toothed whales also possess a full-fledged echolocation system, conceptually quite similar to the system used by boats, although far more sophisticated and powerful. This so-called *biosonar* allows cetaceans to explore the surrounding environment without having to rely on sight—by emitting sound impulses. A rapid series of clicks strikes a target which in turn reflects them; the returning echo supplies the dolphins with a vast range of information concerning the object under examination. Their biosonar (similar to that used by bats) is remarkably efficient—it allows its possessor to locate an object or the intended prey, as well as to evaluate, with considerable accuracy, the distance, based on the time that passes between the emission of the sound and the perception of the

sound's "reflection." Moreover, it enables the cetacean to distinguish the shape of the object in question, and even to verify the material from which it is made. For example, bottle-nosed dolphins are capable—as has been established in aquarium studies—to detect the presence of a small steel sphere just one inch across at a distance of 230 feet. The sounds are emitted through nasal sacs in the cranium and are then amplified by a melon-shaped protuberance, which is an organ, filled with waxy substances, located in the animal's forehead (the cause of the distinctive bulge in the heads of many species).

WHY DOLPHINS GET CAUGHT IN NETS

Each year, thousands of cetaceans die tangled in the drift nets of fishing boats in the open seas. So serious is the situation that there is some risk of the disappearance of entire populations around the world. Although their sight is quite good and they are equipped with biosonar, dolphins, porpoises, and other, similar animals are apparently incapable of avoiding these fatal traps. In an effort to find a solution, a great deal of research has been done. The hypothesis that the nylon filaments used in the drift nets currently in use is invisible to the sonar of the cetaceans has been discarded. In fact, in theory, cetaceans are perfectly capable of perceiving a net at a distance that is quite sufficient to allow it to reverse direction. The most obvious solution is that dolphins may actually "cruise" with their biosonar "turned off," using it only when they are in a hunting mode, since in an area as vast as the ocean they should hardly be in fear of encountering obstacles. Otherwise, they might well perceive the presence of the net but imagine it to be something through which they can easily swim, and therefore they make no effort to avoid it. For this reason, drift nets have been tested that are outfitted with acoustic signals which emit a "warning" sound. They have not been successful, for just how should we warn cetaceans that something is dangerous? Only individual animals that have survived a bad experience are capable of learning lessons from it, and being trapped in the nets almost always means certain death. Also, many cetaceans are specifically attracted by the fish caught in the nets (or by the predators that are in turn attracted by those fish), which means that in all likelihood, they will interpret those sounds as an invitation to lunch. Until now, the conclusions drawn from the research have been unequivocal but by no means encouraging. In all probability, there is no solution to the problem of drift nets, except for the total prohibition of their use in the areas where cetaceans are most commonly found.

EMISSION OF SOUND IMPULSE

RETURNING ECHO

ECHOLOCATION

The sounds used in echolocation (the "clicks") are produced in the nasal sacs and are probably concentrated in the melon, which serves as an "acoustic lens." When the sounds return from the target, they are conveyed to the ear through the channel of fat surrounding the jaw.

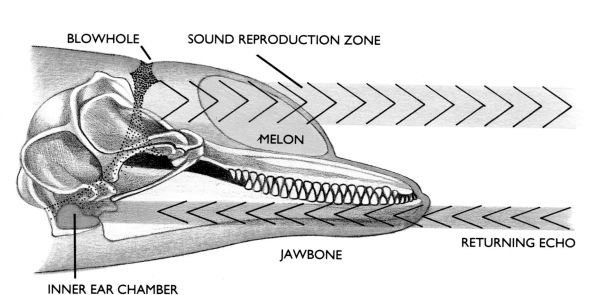

BLOWHOLE   SOUND REPRODUCTION ZONE

MELON

INNER EAR CHAMBER

JAWBONE

RETURNING ECHO

RESEARCH

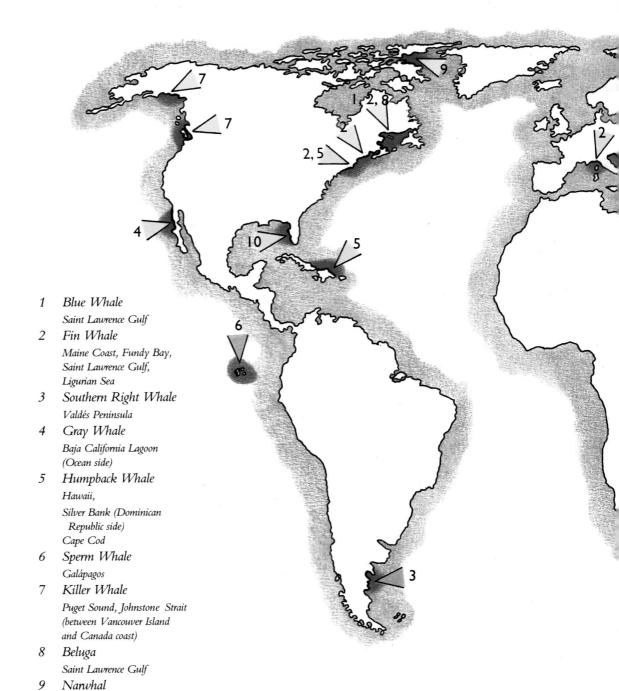

1   *Blue Whale*
    Saint Lawrence Gulf

2   *Fin Whale*
    Maine Coast, Fundy Bay,
    Saint Lawrence Gulf,
    Ligurian Sea

3   *Southern Right Whale*
    Valdés Peninsula

4   *Gray Whale*
    Baja California Lagoon
    (Ocean side)

5   *Humpback Whale*
    Hawaii,
    Silver Bank (Dominican
    * Republic side)*
    Cape Cod

6   *Sperm Whale*
    Galápagos

7   *Killer Whale*
    Puget Sound, Johnstone Strait
    (between Vancouver Island
    and Canada coast)

8   *Beluga*
    Saint Lawrence Gulf

9   *Narwhal*
    Lancaster Sound

10 *Bottle-nosed Dolphin*
    Sarasota Bay, Shark Bay
    Cres and Cossinj (Croatia)

For many centuries, the greatest experts on whales were, paradoxically, also the most ferocious killers of whales. In fact, the biology of cetaceans was studied, during the greatest period of whaling, by dissecting the cadavers of captured whales. Today, the approach to research in this field has radically changed—many of the studies are directed toward the preservation of the species and make use of techniques that are considered nonlethal, which is to say, techniques that do no harm to the animals themselves (with a few depressing exceptions).

In terms of legitimate research, a great deal is done in marine parks and much is learned from the remains of beached animals. Over the last few decades, the most important new discoveries have been the result of observing the animals in their natural environment. Research into the behavior, the social organization, the population dynamics, and so on, has been very

fruitful. This is a field, however, in which researchers encounter enormous difficulties; it is necessary to keep in mind that cetaceans spend most of their time under water, often in the high seas, and in any case in an environment where it is possible to work only during the better seasons. It should therefore come as no surprise that in cetology, more than in other branches of zoology, there are often more mysteries to be solved than there are principles to be enunciated or rules to be codified. Whatever the case, the keystone to modern research on cetaceans has been, perhaps, the so-called technique of "photoidentification." In many species, individual animals can be identified one by one by specific natural markings.

For instance, even though it may seem impossible at first sight, it is possible to distinguish one humpback from another by the black-and-white mottled markings on the lower side of

the fluke. This is the cetacean equivalent of a fingerprint, and it can be photographed and compared with the flukes of other humpbacks. It is unique in every humpback whale, and researchers have compiled entire catalogues of these fingerprints. By taking photographs year after year of the individuals in a certain area, it becomes possible not only to form estimates of the population, but also to reconstruct "biographies" of the individual animals from birth to death. Killer whales, too, can be recognized individually, from their white dorsal spots and from the silhouette of their dorsal fin. In order to understand the organization of the remarkable cetacean population studied along the Pacific coasts, researchers analyzed for years the makeup of the different family groups, identifying a number of individuals. Among fin whales, other identifying traits are used, such as certain faint white markings behind the head, as well as the silhouette of the fins and other signs on the body; right whales are identified by calluses on the heads, bottle-nosed dolphins by notches and other marks on the dorsal fin. Photoidentification is used mainly for the study of groups that always, or periodically, frequent the same area; animals that are less predictable in

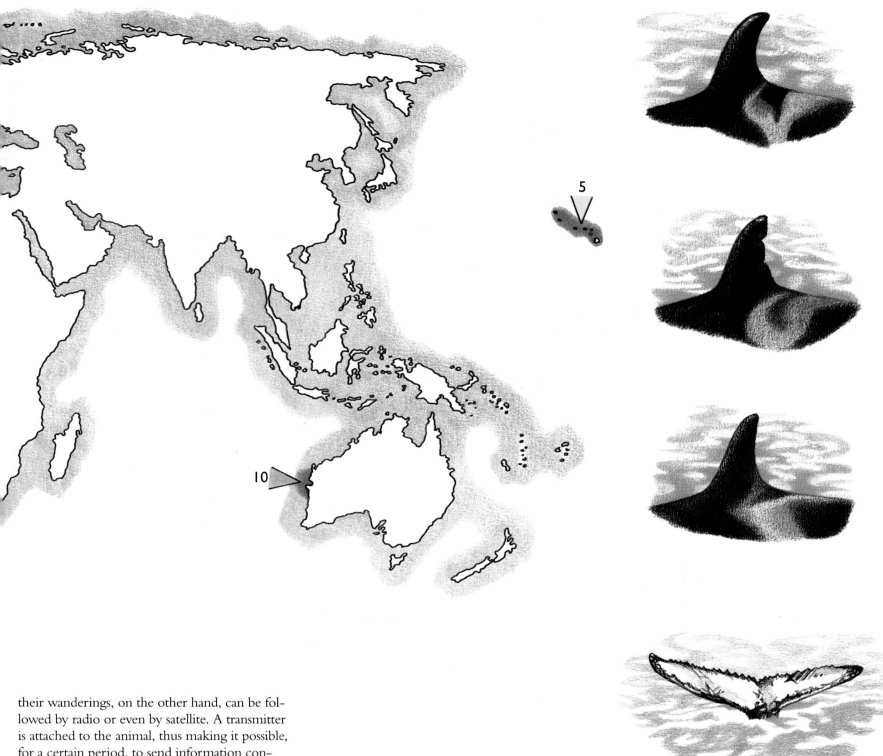

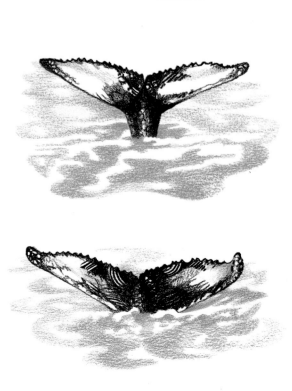

their wanderings, on the other hand, can be followed by radio or even by satellite. A transmitter is attached to the animal, thus making it possible, for a certain period, to send information concerning that animal's movements and activities.

Another characteristic of cetaceans that is used regularly today in research is their tendency to make use of sound in navigation, maneuvering, and in communication. Special hydrophones (underwater microphones) make it possible not only to record the sounds emitted by the animals in an effort to interpret them, but also to establish which species and even the number of individuals to be found hidden in a given stretch of ocean. Bioacoustics has proven to be an invaluable resource, for instance, in the study of sperm whales, which spend long periods of time at great depth, rarely appearing on the surface.

Another field that is now rapidly expanding is genetics. From a small strip of skin, it is possible to determine the gender of an individual animal, and much more. It is possible to establish the degree of resemblance between different populations or the degree of genetic variability that is present in a certain group. Skin samples are gathered, in the case of baleen whales, by firing a crossbow arrow tipped with a small metal cylinder which gouges out a sample and can be recovered by reeling it back in. The same technique can be employed in order to obtain fragments of blubber to be analyzed for possible contaminants. And contaminants are almost always found—lethal chemicals such as DDT and PCB accumulate in considerable quantities in the blubber of cetaceans. This should be an alarming piece of information for humans; cetaceans are closely dependent upon the ocean environment, as we are (like cetaceans, we eat fish and crustaceans). If cetaceans are being slowly poisoned, we can expect serious trouble for our species as well—and this is just one more reason to study our ocean mammal cousins. Another reason is to ensure future generations a healthful ocean abounding in whales, dolphins, and porpoises—some of the most remarkable animals that exist.

PHOTOGRAPHY CREDITS